THE DAY ITALIAN FOOTBALL DIED

THE DAY ITALIAN FOOTBALL DIED

Torino and the Tragedy of Superga

Alexandra Manna and Mike Gibbs

First published in Great Britain byThe Breedon Books Publishing Company Limited
Breedon House, 44 Friar Gate, Derby, DE1 1DA. 1999

This paperback edition published in Great Britain in 2015 by DB Publishing, an imprint of
JMD Media Ltd

ISBN 978-1-78091-480-0

Printed and bound in the UK by Copytech (UK) Ltd Peterborough

Contents

For Maya

With special thanks to

Piero Dardanello
&
Ale Toro magazine

Introductions

ON 5 September 1991, I returned to my home city of Turin after spending two months' summer holiday doing work experience for an Italian company in Solihull, a small English town close to Birmingham. This was my second visit to England. The reason why I used to spend my holiday time in that country was mainly to learn the English language, and I am happy to have done so because now I can tell the amazing story of my home town team, the Torino Calcio Football Club. The Torino club is one of the biggest names in Italian football and, although since the Superga tragedy of 1949 Torino have won only one Scudetto and three Coppa Italia, the Torino supporters are still numbered in their tens of thousands and spread all around the world. Today, as the game of football has become a business much hyped by the media, Torino fans can still maintain some of the traditional values of supporting their club.

On the day I returned to Italy my father told me that he had taken a job with a new local daily newspaper named *La Gazzetta del Piemonte*. He had recently retired from another newspaper, *La Stampa*, where he had worked for 30 years. *La Stampa* is the main daily paper of Turin and belongs to the Agnelli family, the owners of Torino's great rivals, Juventus FC. As he was definitely not the sort of man to sit back, relax and enjoy his pension, my father wished to keep on working. And as he had always been a Torino supporter, there was a special reason why he wanted to work for *La Gazzetta del Piemonte* – the newspaper had been started by the new chairman of the Torino Football Club, an Italian called Gianmauro Borsano. The club had been bought by this unknown businessman very quickly with the deal seemingly happening overnight. Through my father I also started to do some work for *La Gazzetta del Piemonte*. I have always been good at drawing and they asked me to produce sketches for publication. Every day I arrived at the paper's premises only to feel a very strange atmosphere around the place. In my eyes the newspaper was very disorganised; people used to come and go nearly every day, no one knowing when they were going to be paid and for how long their job would last.

Everything gave me the impression that something else was behind Borsano's idea of starting a newspaper in Turin and his decision to buy the team. I never knew if Borsano was a genuine football supporter. What was well known was that he was looking to be elected as an MP and to do so he had to acquire lots of votes from the Turin people. To enhance his public image he needed the support of the mass media, so advertising himself through a local newspaper presented the perfect opportunity.

Borsano frequently visited the Delle Alpi Stadium before the start of the match, standing on the pitch with a microphone telling us all that he would never sell Torino and with him we would make Torino one of the biggest clubs in Europe. Naturally the fans praised him. Thanks to the votes of the Torino fans and public, who believed in him, Borsano gained from them what he wanted – sufficient votes to make him an MP. Then, only one year after opening the newspaper, and with his purpose now fulfilled, he declared himself bankrupt and the paper closed down. Simultaneously he also sold our idol and star player, Gianluigi Lentini, to Milan and despite the Italian and British newspapers reporting at that time that Lentini was sold for £13 million, Borsano and Milan's president, Silvio Berlusconi, never made public the amount of money that the transfer involved. At the time of writing, Borsano was still under investigation by the tax authorities because of matters surrounding the Lentini transfer.

Myself, my father and all the other Torino fans felt betrayed. The club then went on to be bought and sold by various parties, none apparently with the interest of Torino at heart. Consequently, relegation to Serie B soon followed and the once proud Torino were in disarray.

By this time I had moved to England to further my education at Mid-Warwickshire College and the Brunel College in Bristol where I obtained a National Diploma in computer and business studies. Now I had to follow my beloved Torino through my family, newspapers and television. My love for Italian football then led me to open a stall selling Italian football merchandise and it was there that I met my partner, Mike. His love of football naturally led him to develop an interest in the Torino story. As our relationship developed I confided in him my ambition to one day write a book about Torino and in particular the Superga air crash. This tragedy, with the exception of the Manchester United Munich air disaster, is unparalleled in the history of sport. An entire football team and entourage were wiped out in an instant, a great squad of footballers were denied future glories and women and children were left without husbands and fathers. A city and an entire nation felt their grief, and this happened to the club that I love. Now that we have a family and our interests have become mutual we have combined our knowledge to produce this book.

Alexandra Manna

MY FIRST acquaintance with Torino came via *Shoot* magazine in the mid-1970s. At that time soccer mad youngsters were fed a staple diet of Kevin Keegan, Liverpool, Leeds and Manchester United. However, as I grew up I didn't develop any particular liking for any of these clubs as none of them could come anywhere near my true football love for Bristol Rovers. Besides, I never wanted a poster of Billy Bremner on my bedroom wall. Thus I never had a 'second' team other than developing a soft spot for Berwick Rangers in Scotland after having once spent a summer holiday there. So it was with much interest that I noticed *Shoot* had started to feature top European club sides in their colour club focus articles. The European teams always seemed more glamorous and had a certain mystique about them. I remember the time when a team called Torino were featured after winning the Italian title in 1976, mainly because the colour of their kit stood out and because I recognised among their players the centre-forward Graziani, a famous Italian international player who I had seen cause England problems in a televised match.

Almost two decades later, Channel 4 began their coverage of Italian football and I, like many others, became interested in the domestic Italian game. Every aspect appeared cool and stylish, a far cry from the beer-gut mentality that now seemed to beset the culture of the English game. I quickly developed an interest in the whole Italian football scene – the fans, the players and the stadiums – and I was soon able to grasp why Serie A was considered the best domestic league in world football and why England had slipped so far down the international pecking order. At that time, around 1992-93, the Milan of Gullit and Van Basten were the dominant team not only in Italy but also in Europe, whereas Juventus and Inter were, relatively speaking, nowhere. Gazza and Lazio, meanwhile, were in the early stages of what was to become their love-hate relationship. As a result I did not look for a team to follow; to me every game had its own special appeal. Then one Saturday morning the weekly *Gazzetta* programme previewed the forthcoming Turin derby. Torino were not enjoying the best of seasons whereas their city rivals, Juventus, were beginning their climb back to the top having endured a lean decade since the departure of the great Michel Platini. Torino seemed to capture the real mood of the city – they were the 'people's' team while Juventus attracted a different type of following. I have always had a preference for the team I would follow if I lived in another city: Manchester City in Manchester, Everton in Liverpool, Sheffield United in Sheffield, the main reasons being, I suppose, because I support the underdog, reckoning that, rightly or wrongly, there's more passion and emotion within their support. From that moment I rooted for a Toro win and, lo and behold, the following day they defied the odds and beat their oldest and most bitter rivals. Brilliant I thought.

My interest in Torino then expanded dramatically one fateful day when I met Alex. It's not a regular occurrence in England to come across a stall selling Italian football merchandise especially when its proprietor is stunningly attractive and passionate about football. But that's what fate had in store for me and I've been grateful ever since. We talked that day about Torino and Alex recounted with much affection the great matches she had seen in Serie A and the UEFA Cup, and some of the great players like Enzo Scifo, Martin Vasquez and Junior. Like the rest of the club's supporters, she was saddened at their present plight in Serie B but her burning desire and dream of a return to better days was very much evident, just like the huge Toro banner placed in pole position at the stall.

I left that day the proud wearer of a Torino pin badge which has adorned my jacket ever since. As our friendship developed I remembered that old *Shoot* feature and miraculously managed to retrieve it from my parents' loft where it had been gathering dust all those years. I don't think Alex quite knew what to make of it when I gave her the article, but the colour picture of Torino, circa 1975-76 Serie A champions, soon sat proudly above the posters of the Milans, Baggios and Maldinis. We went on to spend some great times at the stall and many customers always seemed curious as to why Torino were the most prominent club on display. But we knew.

On the personal side our relationship grew and we now have a family. We have spent some great times in Italy visiting relatives and watching football, and Turin in particular has become a second home to me. In particular our visit to Turin in early May 1999 for the 50th anniversary of the Superga tragedy will always hold a special memory for me. It was a privilege to be in Turin at this very special and emotional time and to experience at close hand the warmth, humour and passion of the people. It is through our experiences during our time there, and Alex's passion, that we base this book. Through Alex I have been lucky to gain a fascinating insight into a great football club and the history, people, city and culture behind it. It has always been her ambition to bring the name of the Torino Football Club and a particular period of its history to a wider audience. The story is of joy, tragedy, glory and despair. To place it into context we have delved into the present as well as the past and through our personal experiences in and around Turin we bring this story.

Mike Gibbs

The City of the Bull

IT IS late evening, 29 April 1999, and we are aboard an Alitalia scheduled flight from Stansted airport on route to a northern Italian city situated in the region of Piemonte, or Piedmont as the English know it. The Italian name for the city is Torino but, again, it is known in the English language as Turin. The purpose of our trip is to visit our family and to be present during the week-long tributes which are being planned in the city to commemorate the 50th anniversary of the Superga tragedy, the worst disaster ever to befall Italian football. As we prepare for landing we see the familiar motion of passengers folding newspapers and fastening seat belts in eagerness to see friends and loved ones again. To many people on board such rituals are a regular occurrence but as we approach the Caselle airport in Turin, our thoughts are drawn to a plane trip of 50 years earlier. Then, just minutes before they were due to land, the lives of 31 people were tragically lost when their aircraft crashed on the hill of Superga which overlooks the city.

Most of the passengers on that fateful trip were very young, in the prime of their lives and at the peak of their profession. They were the footballers and officials of the Torino Football Club returning from a friendly match in Lisbon. They were not an ordinary team: an incredible period of success had given them the title of *Il Grande Torino* (the great Torino) and they were set to continue to rewrite football history in Italy before destiny cruelly intervened. Their status as famous sportsmen had given them the privilege to travel abroad, something which 50 years ago an ordinary person could only dream about. Nowadays, to the majority of people flying is something taken for granted and has opened up an endless opportunity to experience different countries and cultures. As we begin our descent we keep reminding ourselves of this fact as just under two hours have passed since we set off from London. The noise of the engines becomes louder as we see the runway from the window and we cannot stop thinking of the emotions those footballers would have felt all those years ago. Homeward bound after a successful trip to Portugal, they too would have been looking forward to seeing their families again and sharing with them their experiences of another country. But 50 years ago their world, and the one of those around them, stopped. Their story is why we are here in Turin at this particular time.

Situated on the outskirts, Caselle airport is like that of many European cities, small and unspectacular, with the majority of its customers passing through mainly for business. The small number of tourists who visit Turin each year come mainly to see the fabled Turin Shroud, housed in the Duomo, the 15th-century cathedral in the city centre. Unlike other major cities in Italy, such as Rome and Milan, Turin has little else to offer in the way of tourism apart from some impressive architecture, museums – and football. Much of the city's history in the 20th century has been dominated by the Fiat car company, owned by the Agnelli family and the major focal point for employment. Fiat's success has made it one of the symbols of Turin and its riches have paved the way for the rise of the Juventus Football Club which it has been financing since 1923.

Many of Fiat's employees, like those elsewhere in the city, hail originally from the south, the part of Italy from which most Italians are stereotyped. To many outsiders the mere mention of Italy invokes images of the Mafia and sharply dressed people in designer outfits and sunglasses who do little else all day except eat pasta and olives, while relaxing in beautiful sunshine. The reality here, however, is far removed from the romantic notion portrayed in films and magazines. Turin is a rather grey, industrial city typical of Northern Europe with a climate which varies between that of intense heat in summer to one of freezing in winter when the snow and ice of the nearby Alps can help send temperatures plummeting to well below zero.

The small number of flights into Caselle has enabled us to collect our baggage quickly and as we pass by the grim-faced official at the security check we catch a welcome glimpse of our relatives, Doni and Lino, who have come to pick us up. Our exchanges are typically Italian, with plenty of hugs and kisses, made even more dramatic by the fact that Doni and Lino are seeing our baby daughter for the first time. With night having now fallen, we load our cases into their Fiat Uno, one of the many Fiat cars parked outside and which dominate the city's traffic, another legacy in Turin of the Fiat company. As we make our way to our parents' apartment we already feel that we are in a different country. Everything seems more chaotic and less organised than England, with cars buzzing around everywhere. The tall apartment blocks which dominate the city create a suffocating effect and appear to capture the constant smoke and pollution emanated not only from the incessant stream of cars but also from the trams and buses which run in the city, creating a vacuum effect. The buildings are much different to the familiar two-up-two-down type housing we are more accustomed to in England. The impressive Baroque architecture reminds us of Paris, but like the French city the buildings have been spoilt by years of pollution and the resulting grime which now covers their exteriors.

Unlike the English, most Italian people still smoke heavily, and Lino is no exception, chain smoking throughout our journey. He is Doni's boyfriend and, although they have a baby six months younger than ours, they have yet to marry. They reflect the changing mentality of the new Italian generation who, unlike their elders, are beginning to adapt their culture to the influence of the film and music industries coming mainly from America and the UK. This is apparent as we speed along the road: the music coming from Lino's car stereo is not from Pavarotti as one might be led to expect but from the Irish band U2. The fact that Lino cannot understand the words or meaning of the songs is unimportant and does not prevent him from singing along to them. Unlike Doni, Lino is not Turin-born but comes from the town of Cosenza situated in the region of Calabria, in the south of Italy. He moved to Turin at the age of 18, to do his national service, and having spent a few years in the military he has obtained the title of carabiniere, a similar job to a policeman with the difference being that while the police are, as in England, a civil power, the carabiniere is part of the military. Like many Southerners he has settled in Turin.

Despite the number of cars on the road, we manage to reach our apartment relatively quickly, a feat which owes much to Lino's driving skills and knowledge of short cuts. We are met by all our family who have gathered to greet us, their delight at seeing us for the first time since the previous summer doubled upon setting eyes for the first time on our daughter Maya. Before we unload our cases and eat, we catch up on recent happenings, both in England and Italy. The subject of football is high on the agenda, much to the pleasure of our father, Riccardo, who excitedly points out that his beloved Torino currently occupy one of the Serie B promotion places and are set for a return to the top flight of Italian football. Riccardo has lived in Turin all his life and has supported Torino, or Toro as they are affectionately known, from an early age when, as a child, he first watched the Grande Torino at their original home, the Filadelfia stadium. Although he remains an ardent supporter, he no longer goes to the stadium to watch the team in action, preferring instead to spend matchdays in the comforts of a Torino gentlemen's club, of which he is a member, and from where he watches every Torino game live on a big screen with other members and fellow supporters. His pride in Torino is reflected by the pennant which adorns the wall of the dining room where, between dinner and more conversation, we unwind after our day's journey. Riccardo has been saving a souvenir journal about the Grande Torino from the Turin daily newspaper *La Stampa*, which he presents to us over a glass of Limoncelo, a popular Italian aperitif made from lemon juice.

After freshening up and putting our daughter to bed we decide to go out for a drink. The area where our parents live, Corso Monte Grappa, is about 20 minutes away from the centre by car at night, so we take a taxi to Piazza Castello, part of a number of the grand squares which make up the city centre. Walking around the centre of Turin at night is a pleasant experience as all the shops and bars are well lit up, creating an impressive atmosphere. Many people are content to casually browse at shop windows, particularly in Via Roma, a street where the most chic and designer clothes shops are found. As we take a leisurely stroll, we notice that the city is getting ready for 4 May 1999, the day of the 50th anniversary of the Superga tragedy. In their windows many bars and shops display photographs and pennants of the Grande Torino.

Eventually we stop at the prestigious Cafe Torino in Piazza Castello, a big square surrounded by a portico of shops and bars. The Cafe Torino is the oldest and most exclusive bar in Turin with an atmosphere all of its own. The elegant decor inside the cafe makes one feel as if one is stepping back in time, but as it is a fine spring evening we decide to sit at one of the tables lined outside. In front of the entrance to the cafe, in the middle of the pavement, a large bull, which symbolises the city of Turin, is engraved in burgundy, the official colour of the Torino club. The team is also nicknamed *I Granata* (meaning the Granata), after the semi-precious garnet stone which is burgundy in colour. The word for bull in Italian is *Toro* and the animal has been the emblem of the city for over two millennia. During the reign of the Roman Emperor, Caesar Augustus, a wall was built around the city to protect it against foreign invaders and according to legend, when the Barbarians finally ransacked the city they did so with the help of a giant bull which broke down the city gates. The invaders, remembering the role which the bull had played in helping defeat the Romans, decided to call the new settlement Torino in honour of the animal. The bull can be found everywhere around the city and is also the symbol which appears in the logo of the Torino Football Club. Many Torino supporters attach a sticker of the logo on their car number plate to show their allegiance to the team, and if you pay attention to the cars around you it is an easy thing to spot all over Turin.

As we enjoy a glass of wine, we engage in a spot of people watching, varying from young couples and teenagers to families with children and babies, all comfortable in the fact that in this part of the city at least, they can walk around late at night without fear of intimidation or violence, something we would perhaps not see in England. The main customers of the bar speak with a local Piedmont accent, as unlike Milan or Rome this is not a cosmopolitan city. Their conversations centre mainly around local events and their families, but most of the talk is now revolving around the Grande Torino, particularly among the older people out enjoying a drink for the evening.

As the night begins to draw to its end, our heavy eyes signal that it is time to go back to the apartment. Before leaving, we go into the bar to settle our bill for the evening and while waiting our turn at the counter we see a large framed photograph of the Grande Torino squad under the optics. The saying goes that every picture tells a story and for this particular one the adage speaks the truth. The footballers appear as if they are frozen in time, looking as if they could step out of the frame at any moment. As we take our taxi ride home, we cannot stop talking about this remarkable image we are seeing all around us. The players have become icons, creating their own special niche in the hearts of people not only in Turin but throughout Italy. As we discover more about this extraordinary set of faces it is as if we are taking a step back in time ourselves. To find out where it all began we have to delve even deeper into the past to unfold the origins and development of the Torino club and the legacy which lays beneath the surface of the Grande Torino story.

Early Days

THE modern game of football in Italy, with its multi-million lira contracts, superstars and huge worldwide following, is a far cry from the game of yesteryear, but like the majority of today's commercially exploited sports can trace its genesis to more humble beginnings. Towards the end of the 19th century, a Swiss trader living in Turin by the name of Edoardo Bosio was a frequent visitor abroad. His purpose for travelling was mainly business and it was during such a trip to England that he attended a football match, a gathering of young men kicking a leather ball around a field. Bosio had stumbled across the game by chance and immediately saw its popularity, not just among those who played it but to the extent that crowds would gather to watch. Football was already being played in Italy, the game having been introduced by English sailors in the port of Genoa, but its participants were mainly students. However, as the 19th century drew to an end, football was already well established in England with numerous teams governed by an organised 'Football Association'.

Bosio decided to prolong his stay in England to enable him to take a look at the game in more depth, and on his return to Turin in the spring of 1887 he already had the firm intention of starting an Italian 'football board', the equivalent of the English FA. He discussed his idea with a group of Britons who were working for the Adams Company of Nottingham which had a branch in Turin. The proposal received a very positive response and a few months later they established a sporting club where in the summer climbing and canoeing would be practised, with the rest of the year dedicated purely to football. As a consequence football began to prosper in the city of Turin. In its infancy the game was attracting only male spectators but a few years later, women found an interest in the game. With their growing enthusiasm Edoardo Bosio and his British friends from the Adams Company founded the 'Football Cricket Club' in 1887 and Bosio, along with Beltrami, Weber, Kilpin, Pecco and Savage, became the first footballers to be applauded by the Turin public.

At that time there was a distinction between the working and noble class with the divide being deep enough for the noblemen of Turin to found their own club called 'Nobili'. Among these more distinguished individuals were the Duke of Abruzzi, the Marquis Ferrero of Ventimiglia and the Baron Cesana, all very eminent names of that period. As a result of their actions a fierce rivalry sprang up between the two clubs. Nevertheless, in 1890 both clubs joined together to form the Football Club Internazionale.

The new club organised matches against English sailors working at the port of Genoa. The matches were an opportunity for the club to learn more about the rules of the game and to pick up new technical tips from their English counterparts and as is often the case the apprentices soon overtook their more illustrious teachers. In the spring of 1893 the local papers reported a 2-1 victory by the Football Club Internazionale over the English sailors, the line-up for this momentous victory being: Beaton, Kilpin, Dobbie, Lubatti, Schoenbrod, Pecco, Savage, Nasi, Weber, Beltrami and Bosio. The goals were scored by Weber and Schoenbrod with the English team replying through an own-goal from Dobbie.

This sensational victory against an English team projected football in Italy into a new dimension. By now players were in the early throes of true football fever, to the extent that they were more than willing to dig into their own pockets to provide the finance necessary for their kit and travelling expenses. Eventually this created problems within the Internazionale club with the number of players increasing dramatically due to the new-found popularity of the game. The rise in interest also brought controversy as selection processes were introduced to decide who would play in the games. Initially the decision was taken that only the best players would play but the club soon realised that many of the better players could not afford their own kit and travelling costs. Faced with this dilemma the club had no option but to consider players who, though less talented, were of a sounder financial status.

In 1894, a new team, under the presidency of the Duke of the Abruzzi, was founded named the Football Club Torinese. At their inception everyone assumed that the team was affiliated to the Club Internazionale but it later became evident that there was now an authentic and independent second team in Turin. Alas, although there was enough room for everyone to play, the problem of the rich and poor players had still not been solved. The game of football on an organised level was starting to incur increasing financial expenditure, for beside the cost of kit and equipment, away matches were becoming more numerous, adding to the expense of travel.

Between 1893 and 1894, Torino, Milano, Genoa, Treviso, Alessandria and Palermo were all prominent teams in the vanguard of football in Italy and, after a period in which only friendly matches had been played, the idea of starting an official tournament soon became inevitable (the English FA Cup had started in 1870, the

Football League in 1888). In 1898 the directors of all the Italian clubs met in Turin and together they formed the first Italian Football Federation (*Federazione Italiana del Football*) with the honour of the first presidency of the newly-formed organisation being given to the Count of Ovidio. Among the five teams which joined the Federation were the recently-formed Sport Club Juventus, founded by some Turin students on 1 November 1897, and who at the time sported an all-pink kit.

The first tournament

By the end of the 19th century Turin was a very rich and powerful city, one seen as representative of all Italy, a country that had never previously been considered united. The centre and south of the country were culturally alienated from the north and were extremely poor and so Turin, being an important city at that time, naturally became the football capital of Italy. By this time, besides FC Torinese and SC Juventus, there were two other teams already fairly well established in Turin, the Audace Torino and the Ginnastica Torino. Football, though, still had a very limited number of teams and the game was still being played on squares with no proper grounds from where matches could be suitably watched by the public. The pace of the game began to accelerate when, on 6 January 1898, the Club Torinese played a match against the Genoa Cricket and Athletic Club in Turin, the start of a longstanding bond between the clubs which exists to this day. The Genoa team, formed by British expatriates, had a big reputation for playing football of a very high technical standard but it was the Torinese who won the match with a goal from Savage scored just a few minutes from time.

The first tournament in the history of Italian football took place in Turin on 8 May 1898. The competition started and concluded on the same day and it was Genoa who took the honours emerging victorious over the Club Internazionale. The formidable Genoa team repeated the feat by winning the following two tournaments, again defeating the Club Internazionale on both occasions. Although encountering little success on the pitch, the Club Torinese were able to enjoy the fruits of the tournament when, for the first time, they registered a paying attendance for a football match in Italy, with 115 spectators producing gate receipts of 229 lire, a large attendance and big money in those early days.

On 30 April of that year, the Club Torinese supplied five of its players to an Italian national squad to play a match against Switzerland and although the match was not officially recorded it is generally considered as the first to be played by the Italian national team. Turin was now a city which was producing football of an ever improving standard and with a steady stream of good footballers beginning to emerge, its influence was beginning to spread from domestic to international level. However, although the city's two main teams, Club Torinese and Juventus, were playing an exciting brand of football, the championship was still being dominated by Genoa.

At football entered the new century, the Club Torinese suffered a serious financial crisis, leaving Juventus as the main flag bearer for football in the city. In 1902 the regional championship in Piedmont saw the Club Torinese play out a 1-1 draw against Juventus in a match which took on the feel of a local derby. After beating the Audace Torino 6-0 and the Ginnastica Torino 1-0, the Juventus team faced a second confrontation with the Club Torinese in the semi-final of the competition, winning comfortably 4-1. While Juventus had now established themselves as the leading footballing power in Turin, they were still no match for Genoa who went on to record their fourth title from the five championships contested.

The Club Torinese had been eliminated from the championships of 1903 and 1904 and in 1905 decided to withdraw altogether. The club was disappearing from the public gaze, a situation which was creating a great deal of concern for Turin football in general. Juventus had won the championship in 1905 but without a rival team of an equal technical level, Turin would cease to lead the development of a sport that had made the city such a great focal point of Italy and Europe. A solution seemed far away, especially taking into consideration the extremity of the Club Torinese's financial situation and that as a consequence its directors had lost credibility with the banks.

However, all was not well at Juventus with relations among its directors not being as strong as its financial resources. One of the directors, Alfredo Dick, was a wealthy Swiss manufacturer who was busy accumulating a fortune through leather goods and shoes. His great passion for football had led him to invest money in Juventus. He had previously held the position of president of the club but had been forced to stand down after being accused of trying to 'export' the Juventus club abroad and of changing its name in the German language to 'Jugend Fusballverein'. Dick claimed to have been deeply hurt and insulted by the accusations and together with some other Juventus directors and a few more Swiss and Italian businessmen offered to collaborate financially and technically with the directors of the Torinese Club. In return they asked that a completely new club be reformed to compete against Juventus. The offer made by Alfredo Dick was the only way in which the debts of the Torinese Club could be settled while also guaranteeing the players football under the emblem of a new club. The wheels had been set in motion for the birth of a great rivalry.

A new team is born: Torino Calcio Football Club

On the cold and windy evening of 3 December 1906, the pioneers of the Torino Calcio met in a small private room inside the pub Voigt, situated in a corner between Via Pietro Micca and Via Botero in Turin. As the evening progressed Alfredo Dick became more convinced than ever that a brand new club should be formed. The others were equally in agreement. What they wanted to create was a new and interesting club with a different name and, between glasses of beer and the smoking of cigars, just before midnight a new team was founded in Turin. It was called Torino Calcio Football Club, eventually to become the biggest rivals of Juventus.

The first president of the newly-formed club was elected that evening, despite his not being present. His name was Hans Schoenbrod, a player of modest talent but a man with a great passion for management. Dick decided to leave the responsibility of the club in the hands of Schoenbrod for one year, although later the lure of the position was to prove too enticing and Dick became president himself. In the meantime, Torino Calcio was now well and truly born, its colours having been decided on as burgundy and white.

The club had been quick to announce itself on a verbal level but were now anxious to measure its strengths on the playing side. In 1906 the game in Italy was gradually expanding and was creating a lot of interest throughout the north of the country, although limited among the three regions, Piedmont, Liguria and Lombardia. The debut match of Torino Calcio took place on 16 December 1906 with a friendly against the Pro Vercelli club, the scoreline of 3-1 in Torino's favour ensuring the occasion was marked in suitable style. A year later, in 1907, the founding members of Torino had the satisfaction of beating Juventus in the elimination round of the Piedmont championship, in the first-ever derby match between the two clubs.

In the early stages of the Italian championship the teams contained many foreign players. Their presence was justified by the fact that the game in Italy was still in its very early stages and that their knowledge of rules and tactics would be passed on to the Italian players. However, by 1908, with Italian football now developing its own style and identity, the Federazione Calcio banned teams with a large quota of foreign players from participating in the championship and so the tournament of 1908 went ahead with the absence of Torino, Milan and Genoa. Meanwhile Alfredo Dick had replaced Schoenbrod to become the new president of Torino and under his ruling he put the club back into competitive action by introducing a new all-Italian squad. With their new line-up Torino announced their future intentions, returning to the limelight on 24 January 1909 when they eliminated Juventus from the championship before succumbing to Pro Vercelli, who in turn beat Genoa to capture the title.

Among the best Torino players of this early period was the Turin-born Enrico Debernardi who won three caps for the national team. Debernardi was an attacking right winger and took part in Italy's first official international match when they triumphed 6-2 against France at the Milan Arena on 15 May 1910. On that occasion Italy had played in white shirts and it was not until the following year, in 1911, for a match against Hungary, that the famous blue shirts were worn for the first time. The newspapers reported that they had chosen to play in blue to symbolise the sky of Italy which generally was free from clouds. The reality, though, was that blue was the colour of the Savoy Royal Family and it was not by chance that the Savoy emblem, a shield, was sewn on to the first Italian international shirts. By adopting this colour the national team quickly became known as the 'Azzurri', the Italian word for sky blue.

The arrival of the first Torino coach, World War One and a charismatic Count

Up until now Torino were not under the guidance of a proper coach and tactics were more or less decided among the players. This was to change in 1912 with the appointment of the first recognised coach, Turin-born Vittorio Pozzo, a man who would become symbolic in the history of Italian football and who loved the game more than anything else in life. Under Pozzo the team progressively improved, developing new ideas and strategies, although results remained average. Among the initiatives formulating around the club at this time was a plan to visit South America. Taking into account the complications and expense of such a trip, this seemed an incredible idea. Nevertheless the tour went ahead and in 1914 the club travelled by sea to Brazil where they played six games, winning them all. Returning to Italy, however, the Torino club found that conditions had changed dramatically. World War One had erupted across Europe and domestic football was hardly a priority. Instead the Torino club agreed a contract for a series of games in Argentina. After an awful journey they lost the first fixture of the tour but recovered to beat Nazionale 2-0. With the return journey home equally uncomfortable it was a relieved and happy Pozzo and his squad who were greeted by their families upon arrival at the Port of Genoa.

The war meant there was no longer time for serious football and the Torino players, like all their contemporaries, were called up for active service. Many of those players never returned, among them Biano, the first goalkeeper in the history of Torino who played in the inaugural Turin derby. Most football grounds were taken over for the war effort, with some eventually being destroyed. Five years would pass before competitive football resumed but with so many lives having been lost and with much economic depression, the desire to survive won through and with it football made its comeback with all the vitality and innocence of youth. Pozzo rebuilt the team with a mixture of footballers old and new. Among the emerging players was a distinguished young man of good temperament and great style, the second of four talented footballing brothers. His name was Cesare Martin. Towards the end of 1919, Martin broke into the Torino first-team squad, going on to play over 400 matches and establishing himself as one of the most famous players in the club's history.

With the reintroduction of the Italian championship in 1920-21, the new Torino squad won their first eliminating round to reach the inter-regional stage which opened the door to the semi-finals. The four teams left were Mantova, Padova, Legnano and Torino. At the end of the group matches Torino and Legnano shared equal points meaning that a play-off was necessary with the deciding fixture taking place in late

June at Vercelli. The stifling summer heat made it difficult for the players to breath and the game finished 1-1. After extra-time had brought no further goals, a further two periods were played but again the score remained the same. With both sets of players suffering from exhaustion the clubs decided enough was enough and signalled their intentions with the waving of white flags. Both teams were so tired that they decided against replaying the game and unanimously withdrew from the tournament.

Among the new breed of Torino players contesting this stage of the tournament was an as yet unknown 17-year-old called Antonio Janni who came from the region of Piemont. Pozzo had decided to play the powerful Janni at centre-forward, a decision that paid off handsomely with the youngster going on to remain a fixture in the Torino side for the next 15 years, gaining 23 international caps in the process. Janni's career was to lead Torino through the breakthrough success of the 1920s to the glory of the 1940s.

In the early 1920s many of Italy's smaller clubs were clamouring for an opportunity to compete with the top sides. It seemed a logical step but the impracticalities of organising such a tournament made the idea impossible. By means of a compromise the championship was split into the Lega Nord and Lega Sud, two different competitions for the north and south of the country. Thus, in 1921-22 two championships were disputed. Torino participated in the championship of the north which was organised by the *Confederazione Calcistica Italiana* (CCI) and won by Pro Vercelli while the southern competition of the *Federazione Italiana Gioco Calcio* (FIGC) was won by Novese.

Football was changing rapidly in this period and to cope with the developing game a restructuring took place in the Torino club. In April 1922, after 15 years at the club, Pozzo left due to family reasons and was replaced as coach by an Austrian named Karl Sturmer. To complete the turnaround a new president was elected in the summer of 1924, Count Enrico Marone Cinzano. As well as being a noble figure and lover of sports, Count Cinzano possessed organisational skills in abundance. Although he treated Torino essentially as a hobby, he was able to bring these skills to bear for the great benefit of the club, his first moves coming in the summer of 1925 in the form of two inspirational signings. A host of talented players were beginning to emerge from Alessandria, a town close to Turin, and from this unlikely source Cinzano signed the brilliant Adolfo Baloncieri. The Argentinian Julio Libonatti soon became the next signing and together with Janni formed what would become a magnificent trio.

A new home for Torino Calcio: the mythical Filadelfia stadium

Prior to the arrival of Count Marone Cinzano, Torino had no proper ground to call their own and had been obliged to wander around the city playing at different venues. Marone Cinzano decided to put an end to this nomadic existence by building a stadium for the team, naming it the Campo Filadelfia after the road via Filadelfia where it was situated. The stadium, designed by the engineer and architect Signor Gamba, took less than a year to build and Torino marked the opening match there on 17 October 1926 with a 4-0 victory over the Roman team Fortitudo. Considered ultra-modern in its design, with a character all of its own, the new complex had a capacity of around 20,000 with the open concrete terraces complemented by an aristocratic-looking wooden stand. The fans were quick to nickname the stadium the 'Fossa dei Leoni', meaning the Lion's Den. For them, the Filadelfia was to become a sacred place and their temple of worship, so much so that it became a tradition among the more ardent supporters to watch the players in daily training there. The Filadelfia was soon to enter not only in the legend of the Torino story but also the history of Italian football.

Lo Scudetto

Torino had gradually developed into one of the strongest sides in Italy and with the vital components now in place on and off the field, in 1926-27 they claimed their first championship, Lo Scudetto. The Scudetto referred to the shield which represented the symbol of the Savoy Royal family and was a name soon to become an integral part of the Italian vocabulary. The championship now comprised 20 teams divided into two groups, and the top six teams – Bologna, Inter, Milan, Genoa, Torino and Juventus – contested the final group which was won by Torino in exciting fashion. The title for which they had been so desperately striving was now theirs, but events were to take a dramatic turn. No sooner had the championship been won than it was taken away by the Federation after allegations that a Juventus player named Allemandi had been bribed. An enquiry revealed that Allemandi had been offered an undisclosed sum by one of the Torino directors, Dr Nani, to help Torino win the second leg of the derby on 5 June 1927 (they won 2-1). The accusation that Allemandi accepted the money was never proven but the scandal was strong enough for the club to be stripped of the title and, amid great despondency, there came the realisation that they would have to start all over again.

With an overwhelming desire to claim back what had momentarily been theirs, Torino captured the title in the following 1927-28 season, recovering from a bad start to overtake Genoa and take the championship officially for the first time. Inspired by the gifted trio of Baloncieri, Libonatti and Rossetti, and with Janni at centre-forward, Torino produced some magnificent performances culminating in some incredible results including wins of 11-0 against Napoli and Brescia and 14-0 against Reggiana. This time there was no disputing the fact that the tricolour truly belonged to the Granata. With such a strong squad now assembled, a great feeling of optimism emanated from players and fans alike and the wonderful line-up of Bosia, Monti III, Martin II, Martin III, Colombari, Speroni, Vezzani, Baloncieri, Libonatti, Rossetti II and Franzoni was enough to convince most observers that Torino were about to enter a great cycle of success. Luck, however, was to desert them the following season when, despite ending up in the Final against Bologna, they were defeated by a solitary goal and were resigned to second place.

The start of Serie A and triumph in the Coppa Italia

The continuing progress that football was making in Italy led to another fundamental change in the organisation of the championship in 1929-30 when the Federation decided that only one major tournament should be played. The new structure was to allow the championship to take place on a national level with clubs competing from all over Italy, providing that they were of a suitable size and financially stable. The smaller clubs were left to compete in a minor tournament from where a winning route would allow them to take their place automatically in the major tournament. The new league system had begun, with the new title of Serie A afforded to the major tournament.

The transformation of the Italian game's infrastructure coincided with a long period of crisis for the Torino club with the 1930s bringing a different kind of experience to players and fans alike. A number of established players, including Baloncieri, Rossetti II, Libonatti and Janni, were allowed to leave prematurely with their places taken by younger players and new signings, including some foreign players notably from South America. As the decade wore on, the fans were forced to endure growing performances of mediocrity as the Torino squad became more and more affected by the continuing change in management and tactics. Between 1928 and 1939 many presidents and coaches came and went with the team suffering from the revolving door policy which was enveloping the club. Things were not made any easier when great rivals Juventus entered centre stage, winning five consecutive titles between 1930 and 1935, the new-found dominance of their most bitter adversaries only adding to Torino fans' woes. Although everything seemed to conspire against them, there was still something to savour in the form of some talented players emerging from the youth team, known as the Balon Boys. Most of them decided to stick with Torino instead of opting to play for other Serie A teams. It was a collective decision that would serve Torino well over the coming years and one that the rest of Serie A would live to regret.

Before the new breed of young players could make their mark a major crisis had to be averted. In 1934-35, the last of the five-year period of Juventus winning the Scudetto, the Serie A tournament was made up of 16 teams and, although starting the season with a reasonable squad, Torino plummeted down the league table to find themselves in bottom place. On the last day of the season, 2 June 1935, Torino faced Livorno at the Filadelfia. Livorno were on 24 points, one point above them in the table. The situation was simple: anything other than a win would mean relegation to Serie B and possible obscurity. With 20 minutes of the match remaining, and with the atmosphere becoming increasingly intense, Filippo Prato, one of the players promoted from the youth team, scored a magical goal to save Torino from relegation and condemn Livorno, the team from Tuscany, to Serie B along with Pro Vercelli.

The scare suffered that day made everyone connected with the Torino club determined that the experience would not be repeated. Indeed, it acted as the catalyst for a far more successful season in 1935-36 when a final finish of third place was achieved behind Bologna and Ambrosiana. Winning the Scudetto had proved beyond Torino but rich compensation came in the form of the Coppa Italia which was lifted in emphatic style with a 5-1 win against Alessandria in Genoa. With this first triumph in the cup competition, silverware was now proudly back on display, a welcome sign of better things to come.

The Voigt pub, between Via Pietro Micca and Via Botero, Turin, where the Torino club was founded on 3 December 1906.

Left: The first laws and regulations of the Torino club; *top right* Vittorio Pozzo (right), the Torino coach pictured with Enrico Bachmann 1920; *bottom right* Count Marone Cinzano, charismatic president 1924-28 and founder of the Filadelfia Stadium.

Count Marone Cinzano and his Torino squad being introduced to the Prince of Piedmont prior to a friendly against Pro Vercelli in 1926.

The magnificent trio of Libonatti, Baloncieri and Rossetti.

Vincenzo Bosia, goalkeeper of the first Torino Scudetto-winning side 1927-28.

The Making of a Super Squad

T HE winds of war sweeping across Europe in the autumn of 1939 were to have a profound effect on football throughout the continent. Italy, under the dictatorship of Benito Mussolini, did not enter the war until June 1940. However, a time of great uncertainty led many Italians to take comfort in things that were closest to them with the result that football remained high on people's agenda. This fact was exploited by Mussolini's propaganda advisers who argued to the dictator that his country's footballers were of more use on the pitch rather than on the battlefield and consequently were spared being called into active service. For many Italians, football thus remained business as usual and for the Torino club the period marked the appointment of a remarkable man as the new president of the club.

Ferruccio Novo, the man who pulled the strings

Born in Turin on 2 March 1897, Ferruccio Novo was a businessman of middle class upbringing who, in tandem with his brother, was running his own company, manufacturing leather goods. From early childhood Novo had developed a strong passion for football and especially for his beloved team Torino. In 1913, at the age of 16, he had joined the club's youth team as a full-back but modest talent had thwarted his progress and prevented any opportunity of making a career in the game as a player. Undaunted by his own lack of playing ability, Novo slowly began to work his way up the ladder of infrastructure at the club. He was blessed with natural confidence and a strong inner belief, factors which had served him well during previous spells as manager and board member. These same characteristics were also instrumental in helping his election to the prime position within the club, that of president. In pursuing his goal Novo had realised his ambition and become the most influential figure at Torino.

From the start of his reign Novo made it clear that the management of the club would revolve around the decisions of himself and a few carefully hand-picked board members, most of whom were close personal friends. Committing himself to improving the precarious financial situation that had arisen following the departure of Count Marone Cinzano, Novo was anxious to build a strong base from which the club could move forward. For the new Torino to succeed the name of the game was organisation. Delving deeply into knowledge gained from his old contemporary Vittorio Pozzo and from the influential English clubs such as Arsenal which were shaping the game in the 1930s, his first task in rebuilding the playing side of the club was to appoint as coach the Hungarian-born Ernest Egri Erbstein.

By using the English clubs as a role model Novo decided to establish a squad similar to that of an industrial firm. By assigning responsibilities to different people who had their hearts in Torino, he intended to build a club based on loyalty and trust and one which would be totally united in its cause. Among those offered positions in the new set-up were Antonio Janni and Giacinto Ellena, both former players who had shown much loyalty during great careers at the club. The administrative responsibilities of the club were placed in the hands of Rinaldo Agnisetta, an accountant who was running a transport company, and as his personal assistant Novo employed the services of Roberto Copernico, the owner of a cloth shop in the city centre of Turin. The role of youth-team coach was assigned to an Englishman, Leslie Lievesley, who would later be promoted to first-team coach together with Erbstein. All appointees were good friends of Novo's and with the key individuals now in place off the field, he set about using his footballing contacts and acumen to make the necessary additions to the playing staff.

Although the Torino squad featured several talented players such as the goalkeeper Aldo Olivieri, already a World Cup winner, and Sergio Piacentini, it was not yet ready to win the Scudetto. The fine tuning of the team began in earnest with the purchases of Franco Ossola and the Fiorentina player Romeo Menti. After finishing seventh in the 1940-41 championship, which was won by Bologna, Novo strengthened the squad further by buying three players from Juventus: the goalkeeper Alfredo Bodoira, nicknamed 'Forceps' because of his giant hands, and two attackers – the highly talented centre-forward Guglielmo Gabetto and Felice Borel, who took the nickname of 'little butterfly' due to the graceful manner in which he ran.

The team was gradually taking shape but despite playing some exciting football in 1941-42 had to eventually settle for second place behind Roma. With success tantalisingly close, Novo realised that the team was still missing that vital ingredient to turn potential into a winning formula and started on another acquisition campaign in readiness for a new challenge in 1942-43. To the array of talent already at his disposal he added the wing-half pairing of Ezio Loik and Valentino Mazzola from the Venezia club and Giuseppe Grezar from Triestina, all established players eager to maximise their potential with Torino. The planning and ambition shown by Novo worked to great effect and once again, after a 15-year absence, the colours of the Granata decorated the Scudetto. That season was the start of the glory of the squad which in Italian football would become known as Il Grande Torino.

Not content to sit back and admire his achievements, Novo pressed on, making further additions to the squad. His vision was one of continued success. More than anything he wanted Torino to keep winning and dominate the game in the way that Juventus had done the previous decade. In many respects Novo was ahead of his time, his vision for the future easily outstripping that of his contemporaries. During the war years, although the championship was still being contested, the directors of rival clubs had been unwilling to invest any substantial funds, preferring instead to see how the development of the war would affect their interests. Novo wisely took advantage of this situation of unease and was able to purchase the players he wanted at reduced fees. While others had dallied or remained cautious, Novo had acted. In this way he had cleverly stolen a march on his rivals.

During the following seasons under his guidance, Torino went from strength to strength, boosted further by more signings as the side continued its evolution. New arrivals included goalkeeper Valerio Bacigalupo, full-backs Aldo Ballarin and Virgilio Maroso and midfield players Mario Rigamonti and Eusebio Castigliano. Completing the picture in 1948-49 came Rubens Fadini, goalkeeper Dino Ballarin (brother of Aldo), Pietro Operto and Emile Bongiorni. All of these players were to form the mythical Grande Torino, masterfully created and put together by the grand footballing architect, Ferruccio Novo.

The introduction of the WM System

A key innovation in the success of the Grande Torino squad was the development of a method of play known as the WM system. The tactic had been invented by the English coach Herbert Chapman, manager of the great Arsenal side of the 1930s. The system was used by the England team and was first brought to the attention of observers in Italy during an international match in Milan on 13 May 1939 when the two countries fought out a 2-2 draw. The tactic made an impression on Felice Borel who played in the match and who introduced the idea to the Torino club. It was known as the WM system due to the impression given by the two capital letters when giving the disposition of the players in the field. The standard tactic previously used, known as the method system, consisted of a 2-5-3 formation and had been used for years but the tactic had become rigid and predictable. The introduction of the WM system allowed a more flexible approach, encouraging players to play more to their individual strengths. The system was in effect a 3-4-3 formation, the W indicating the defensive part of the team which now composed an additional central defender alongside the two full-backs who were now able to mark their opposing wingers more tightly. This had come about after the alteration to the offside law in 1925. In front of them were two covering defensive midfield players with licence to move forward when appropriate. The attacking part of the team was the M, representing the two attacking midfielders inter linking with the two wingers and centre-forward.

The merits of using the WM system were discussed at great length by Borel, Roberto Copernico and Ferruccio Novo on the evening of 18 December 1941, a meeting which lasted into the early hours. Although Borel only played that one season for Torino, his name became historically linked with the club for his influential opinion on the tactic. After great debate it was agreed that the system be adopted and it was first used during the 1-1 draw against Genoa on 21 December 1941. The system was successfully used for the remainder of the 1941-42 season and was instrumental in Torino achieving second place in the championship. However, the method system was still being used by the national team and Vittorio Pozzo managed to persuade Novo that it would be in the best interests of Italian football to revert back to the tried and trusted tactic.

Alas, the reintroduction of the method system to the Torino squad had a disastrous effect in the opening two matches of the 1942-43 campaign which were lost to Ambrosiana 1-0 and Livorno 2-1. The next match was against Juventus and with Novo unable to contemplate losing the derby, the WM system was reintroduced with the result being a resounding 5-2 win to Torino, all the evidence that was required for the system to remain thereafter.

Ernest Egri Erbstein, a man ahead of his time

Although Ferruccio Novo was the undoubted mastermind behind the Torino club and the team known as the Grande Torino, there were others, too, whose contributions to the success were considerable. Among them was the Hungarian-born Ernest Egri Erbstein, a man steeped highly not only in knowledge and strategies on the football field but also in life itself. Erbstein was born in 1898 at Nagy Varad, today known as the town of Oradea in Transylvania, previously part of Hungarian territory. He started his career in football at Budapest were he found employment working in a stockbroker agency. In the capital he played football for the Budapest club, supplementing an already busy life by studying and obtaining a national diploma in physical exercise. In 1924 he obtained a job in Italy, at the town of Fiume, and consequently signed a contact with the Vicenza club before his penchant for travelling next took him to the United States where he played for a year for the Brooklyn Wanderers of New York in the American Soccer League.

Upon his return to Hungary he began the transition from player to coach, carefully studying the way the game was evolving, a fact not lost on some observers considering that the game and most of its major protagonists originated from England. In 1928 Erbstein received an offer from the Italian club, Bari, having made a favourable impression in Italy in his time there as a player. After a spell with Bari he gained further coaching experience in Puglia, Cagliari and Nocerina before returning to Bari once more. However, it was with the Lucchese club that he started to make a name for himself when, in 1936-37, he guided his previously unfancied team to seventh place in Serie A following successive promotions. For his achievements with them, Erbstein's name remains embodied to this day in the hearts of Lucchese followers alongside that of President Della Santina, the inspiration behind the construction of the current stadium, Porta Elisa.

Erbstein's success with Lucchese caught the attention of Ferruccio Novo who decided that he was the right man to continue the evolution of his great Torino side. However, while his coaching abilities were bringing great professional reward, any personal satisfactions were countered due to the ever-growing political climate. Erbstein was descended from a Jewish family, and after joining Torino with great expectations in 1938 he managed to work for only six months before events unfolded which led to another world war and the persecution of the Jewish people in Europe. Erbstein was forced to flee the country and the journey with his family to Northern Europe was not without great difficulty. In trying to reach Holland, where he had a job offer in Rotterdam, his passport was confiscated by the German police.

Fearful of the immediate future, he contacted the Torino directors to request more documentation which eventually arrived after a long month of waiting. However, even with new documents he was prevented from entering Holland and was obliged to return to Budapest. Despite the hardships of the war, Erbstein managed to keep in contact with Novo until 1944 when during the Nazi occupation he became interned in a prison camp. Incredibly, Erbstein managed to escape imprisonment and after a long and arduous journey eventually reached Italy where he became reacquainted with Novo and the Torino club, this time in happier circumstances.

Like millions of others Erbstein's life and attitudes had been harboured by the war years. Spurred on by an everlasting feeling of survival Erbstein was quick to set about using his experience by reshaping the football ideology within the Torino club. To the Grande Torino, Erbstein was the figurehead responsible for deciding the strategy and function of the entire squad. He was the first Torino coach to allow a more relaxed relationship with the players, overturning the more common authoritarian methods employed by most coaches of that and other eras in favour of a more friendly attitude to earn the players' respect. Among the advice he instilled into the players was the importance of preparing for games correctly, citing the need to adhere to the strict diets which were imposed on the players and the need to rest properly. Erbstein was not slow in recognising ways to maximise performances and with a diploma in sport he possessed a knowledge of the anatomy and workings of the human body. On the coaching side he knew exactly what kind of training was beneficial to each player, recognising the different roles of defenders and attackers. In this respect he was a coach ahead of his time, duplicating the same kind of vision for the game as Novo.

He did not condone violence on the field, believing instead that the game should be played in an elegant way and that winning should come as a result of style and hard work and not brutality. To Erbstein the game was not just about winning but performing with style and it was important that his players did not incite the opposition in any way. In short, he wanted the Grande Torino to have a superior level of behaviour on the pitch, also advising his players that if provoked they should just smile and never attempt to react. Likewise he encouraged them to act in the same manner towards referees if decisions went against them. Erbstein's methods soon became popular with the players who were quick to reciprocate the respect shown towards them, so much so that they would always confide in him with any personal problems.

Erbstein was such a deep thinker that he considered the game of football as a moral duty. Coupled with his behavioural skills lay a mind like a reference point for everyone in the team, both on a physical and psychological level, a true football genius. Although he introduced new training methods that were unknown in Italy at the time, he still remained a studious observer of all aspects of the game, adhering deeply in the main to the roots of most known methods and tactics. By nurturing close personal relationships with the players he was able to make each of them aware exactly what was expected on the pitch. He initiated warm-up exercises before each match and imposed strict discipline in the squad by introducing a fine system of 50 lire to any player who did not follow his rules. He was also one of the first coaches to realise the importance of movement off the ball. Erbstein's influence on the training ground encouraged an already great side to mature and improve even further, with well-established internationals responding to a man touched by genius in his profession and a compassion gained through his life experiences.

An Englishman called Leslie Lievesley

Among the many influential and talented individuals at the Campo Filadelfia in the late 1940s stood an unlikely figure, that of an Englishman by the name of Leslie Lievesley. A pioneer in coaching and training techniques, Lievesley was born at Slaveley, a small town in the county of Berkshire, on 23 June 1911. He began his passage in football as a midfield player for Crystal Palace before his playing career was interrupted by the onset of World War Two in which he served as a paratrooper. When the war ended, Lievesley, at the age of 34, turned his attention to coaching and resurrected his football career with the Dutch national team. Under his guidance they achieved some good results and his progress in Holland was noted by Torino who offered him employment as coach to their youth team in 1947 alongside Carlo Rocca. Lievesley soon impressed and it was no surprise when he was promoted in the following 1948-49 season to work with the first team alongside Egri Erbstein.

Novo regarded Lievesley as a somewhat reserved individual, although he also noted the Englishman's generosity and all-round pleasant demeanour. Working closely with Erbstein, Lievesley became a hard task master, leading by example by being the first figure at the training ground each morning. With the Grande Torino squad he developed the first concepts of the modern methods of training, combining strength work with stretching while also concentrating on improving the players' agility and techniques. All this was new to the champions of the Grande Torino and occasionally they would protest against some of his training methods, although they always respected him.

Lievesley was held in sufficient esteem to be asked by the national coach, Vittorio Pozzo, to assist the Azzurri at the 1948 Olympic Games in London. And with a growing reputation and a desire to become his 'own man', Lievesley was approached by Juventus who offered him a position as their coach for 1949-50. The decision, made by Juventus officials on 31 March 1949, was supposed to be kept secret until the end of the season but the press soon got hold of the story and when the news broke on 13 April 1949, the Torino officials had little choice but to confirm the facts. In a relatively short time Leslie Lievesley had made a remarkable ascent up the football ladder but tragically was never able to fulfil his ambition.

Ferruccio Novo, architect and mastermind of the Grande Torino.

Novo (left) and Roberto Copernico.

The WM system – 1948-49 style.

Bacigalupo

Ballarin   Rigamonti   Maroso

Grezar   Castigliano

Loik   Mazzola

Menti   Gabetto   Ossola

The Hungarian-born coach
Ernest Egri Erbstein.

Ernest Egri Erbstein.

Mario Sperone supervising a training session at the Filadelfia, with Mazzola and Loik at the front of the group.

Leslie Lievesley putting the goalkeeper Bacigalupo through his paces during a training session at the Filadelfia.

The Englishman Leslie Lievesley.

The Invincibles

ALTHOUGH Novo and Erbstein were rapidly formulating a system for success off the pitch, if their ambitions were to turn into reality, there still remained the none too small issue of assembling the right playing personnel. For the club to gain the success he so desired, Novo needed a group of strong, talented footballers of varying temperament and character that would gel together into a potent football force. By cleverly using his considerable business acumen and expertise in the transfer market, and nourishing the existing talent at his disposal, Novo managed to combine the vital components of youth, experience, flair and passion into the players he brought to the club. These were the men who made up a most amazing squad.

The goalkeeper

Valerio Bacigalupo, the man with wings

The first line of defence for the Grande Torino between 1945 and 1949, Valerio Bacigalupo was born at Vado Ligure near Savona on 12 March 1924. He began his career with Cairese, followed by Savona and then Genoa before joining Torino for 160,000 lire. His debut in Serie A came on 14 October 1945 against Juventus, lining up with the famous full-back pairing of Ballarin and Maroso who also made their debuts in the same match which ended in a 2-1 defeat. Despite the disappointing start, Bacigalupo went from strength to strength, firmly establishing himself as the guardian of the Torino goal.

The critical moment of his career occurred in 1946-47 when he injured his shoulder and had to relinquish his position to his deputy, Piani. Once he had regained fitness, Bacigalupo was forced to wait to reclaim his place due to the fine form shown by Piani and suffered in silence during training where he worked harder than ever in an attempt to force his way back into the team. Many of his teammates often saw him crying on the training field but the great character and resilience he demonstrated was rewarded with a recall. A series of outstanding performances during the latter part of the season enhanced his growing reputation and propelled him into the reckoning for the national team for whom he made the first of his five international appearances in a 3-1 win over Czechoslovakia on 14 December 1947.

As a goalkeeper Bacigalupo was very agile, his modest character belying a revolutionary style between the posts. His endearing personality made him a very popular figure with fans and press alike, particular for his ability to save penalties for which he attributed his success rate to a secret method that he had devised. Being a perfectionist, Bacigalupo could not tolerate mistakes, often making dramatic gestures in front of his teammates whenever his goal had been breached. Such an occasion happened during the match between Italy and France in Paris where, with Italy winning 3-0, he became extremely agitated when the French reduced the deficit. His dramatics led even French reporters to define his actions as 'the authentic desperation of an exhibitionist', comparing him to a comedian or a dramatic actor without realising that the attitude shown by Bacigalupo was in keeping with his character and one of sincerity and spontaneity.

Away from football, Bacigalupo preferred to live in Genoa rather than Turin. He was very close to his family, and when told that Torino wanted him to become their new goalkeeper he showed little enthusiasm for the move. However, as soon as he met Martelli and Rigamonti he changed his mind about Torino and the three became close friends. Bacigalupo believed everything that his friend Rigamonti told him, so much so that he often became the butt of jokes from his teammates. However, on the field it was a different story and his haul of four consecutive Scudettos told its own story together with 137 appearances with only 115 goals conceded.

The Full-backs

Virgilio Maroso, the kid

Virgilio Maroso was born at Marostica, a small town close to Vicenza, on 26 June 1925. He was the son of a Swiss immigrant and after his birth his family moved to Turin where his father found employment in a factory. As a child, Virgilio would spend his mornings at school and then the afternoons working in the factory with his father. During his spare time the young boy played football in the field close to his home and one day, while enjoying a kick-around, he was noticed by a coach of the Fiat sporting group who invited Maroso to join the youth team he was running.

Suitably impressed by Maroso's talent, the coach offered two lire if he could juggle the ball ten times on his head. This was a feat easily accomplished as Maroso was able to repeat the skill 30 times. Soon afterwards, a scout for the Torino club noticed him and bought him for 100 lire, a fee which more than repaid the time and investment shown by the Fiat coach.

Before becoming a member of the Torino first-team squad, Maroso was loaned to the Alessandria club in 1943-44, although he did not play during the war championship of that year. Immediately after the liberation he returned to Turin where he became the youngest player in the squad for the 1945-46 season. His debut in Serie A was on 14 October 1945, when he was pitched straight into the frenzied atmosphere of the derby match against Juventus, which proved disappointing as Torino lost 2-1. His displays at full-back were a major factor in the defensive strength of the team and his wholehearted performances, matched with style and precision, were greatly admired by teammates and fans alike. In his four seasons with Torino, Maroso made 103 appearances and scored one goal, his solitary strike coming against Triestina in a 6-0 win on 28 December 1947. He also managed one goal in seven appearances for the national team for whom he made his debut on 11 November 1945 in a thrilling 4-4 draw against Switzerland.

Aldo Ballarin, the tough guy

Aldo Ballarin, together with Maroso, formed a fine full-back pairing for the Grande Torino. The understanding between the two was reflected in similar career paths with both men playing for Torino during the four seasons from 1945 to 1949. Ballarin also made his debut for Torino at the same time as Maroso, against Juventus, and for the national team also, in the 4-4 draw against Switzerland in 1945. Born at Chioggia, a town close to Venice, on 10 January 1922, Ballarin began playing football for his school at the age of 11. On leaving school he joined the small Adria Football Club where he played as a left winger before an injury to a colleague led the club to ask him to play temporarily at full-back. Although he could still adapt some of the abilities he had acquired as an attacker into his game, Ballarin soon realised that the position of full-back was more suitable to him.

Settling into his new position he joined the Rovigo Football Club from where he was spotted by the Triestina club whom he joined in the 1940-41 season, making his Serie A debut against Lazio (0-0) on 26 October 1941. Playing for Triestina, Ballarin once again demonstrated his versatility, albeit under tragic circumstances. On 14 December 1941 the Triestina centre-forward Cergoli died in an accident and Ballarin was asked to fill the striking role for five matches until a replacement was found. In the meantime Ferruccio Novo was forming his Torino team player by player and Ballarin became another piece in the jigsaw when he was signed in 1945 for a then record price of 1,500,000 lire (300,000 lire more than had been paid for Mazzola and Loik). When he joined Torino, the coach Ferrero instructed him that as a full-back his duty was to mark his opposite winger at all times. However, as a former winger himself, Ballarin found it difficult to stick to one part of the pitch and his eccentric attitude and hot temperament invariably led to some clashes with the coach. Although he did not enjoy the same freedom that he had found when playing for Triestina, Aldo Ballarin became an integral part of the Grande Torino and, despite differences over the nature of his role, made 148 appearances, scoring four goals. His ability was also rewarded with nine appearances for the national team.

Sauro Toma, the survivor

Due to an injury, Sauro Toma did not travel with the rest of his teammates to Lisbon and subsequently became the only player from the Grande Torino first team to survive the Superga tragedy. Toma was born on 4 December 1925 at La Spezia, a city in the region of Liguria. Equally adept at filling the roles of full-back and centre midfield, he began his career with his hometown team who took the same name of the city. In the 1942-43 season Spezia loaned him to the Rapallo club for whom he played in the regional championship and made 20 appearances. The following season, 1943-44, he played for Entella and then in 1944 appeared in the war championship with the Borgotaro club. When the championship was resumed following the war, Toma found himself playing in Serie B with Vogherese, for whom he made 22 appearances before returning to Spezia in 1946-47 to play a further 40 matches in Serie B. Although not performing in the highest league, his displays did not go unnoticed and in the summer of 1947 Ferruccio Novo called him into to his Torino squad.

Torino handed him his debut in Serie A on 28 September 1947, in a 6-0 win over Lucchese. During the season he proved to be a more than an able deputy for Virgilio Maroso, playing in 24 matches and becoming a much-respected member of the squad. His joy at winning the Scudetto was curtailed in the following 1948-49 season when, after playing in only two matches, he suffered a bad injury to his left knee. It was a blow which forced him to spend a long time on the sidelines after being advised by the club doctor to take a complete break from the game. The injury prevented him from taking the flight to Lisbon but in the aftermath of the tragedy he continued to play for Torino, remaining the last playing link with the Grande Torino.

Each one of his 14 appearances in 1949-50 were emotional occasions but they were also to be his last for Torino as he suffered a new injury the following campaign. In 1951-52 he regained fitness and was loaned to Brescia in Serie B where he played 26 matches before moving on again the following year to Carrara. His nomadic playing career continued with two seasons at Bari for whom he played in 1953-54 and 1954-55. Although appearing in only 26 matches for the Grande Torino, his name has become synonymous with the club. He is now a writer and, as such, an authentic voice on the tragedy, remaining the emblem and testimony of the squad once regarded among the best in the world.

The stopper

Mario Rigamonti, the rock

Mario Rigamonti was born at Brescia on 17 December 1922. He played for Lecco and his hometown team Brescia as a centre-midfielder, starting his Brescia career at the age of 15 while still at school. Rigamonti was not a conscientious student and regularly missed school, more often than not to play football. Concerned about their son's attitude towards his education, his parents decided to send him to Turin to attend a private school which enjoyed a good reputation for turning wayward pupils into model pupils.

Moving to Turin, Rigamonti found himself without a team and quickly began to make friends with a few local footballers. The Torino club had scouts all over the city, with the majority of them being former players of the club, one of whom was Mario Sperone. One day a friend introduced Rigamonti to Sperone, who decided to give him a trial. Although the young Mario had started his career as a right winger and had later become a centre-forward, he was played in defence in the trial. The scout was impressed by his performance, deciding that this was his natural position, and the following year, 1940, Torino reached an agreement with Brescia and paid the sum of 25,000 lire for the option to buy him.

Before becoming reserves for the Torino squad, it was common practice for all young hopefuls to be sent to play in a smaller team called Taurina. However, during the war Rigamonti had to leave for national service and in 1943 he returned to Brescia to play for them once more before moving to Lecco in 1945 while waiting for the war to end. When peace was restored, there were a few directors among the Torino club who were in favour of allowing Rigamonti to join the Lecco club permanently as there were already five midfielders in the squad. However, Novo and a fellow director Agnisetta rejected the idea and immediately requested Rigamonti's return to Turin.

Along with several other notable players, Rigamonti, taking the place of the injured Santagiuliana, made his Serie A debut on 14 October 1945 in the 2-1 defeat by Juventus at the Stadio Comunale. Despite being considered a reserve, he soon established himself as the number one midfielder in the squad. He could use both feet, was good in the air and as the central defender had the responsibility of breaking up opposition attacks. Although his style did not endear him to spectators, he soon developed into the perfect stopper.

Off the pitch Rigamonti was a rebel who loved nothing better than riding his motorbike. On occasions he would disappear for days on end. For Serie A matches, he had a bad habit of turning up at the stadium just minutes before kick-off but Novo always forgave him for his indiscretions and allow him to take his customary position in the centre of defence. He shared a flat in via Nizza with Bacigalupo and Martelli, with whom he liked spending his time in bars around the city centre, and the three became known as the 'trio Nizza'. Despite his rebellious image, Rigamonti went on to become one of the driving forces behind the success of the Grande Torino, making 140 appearances and scoring one goal. He was rewarded with his international debut on 11 May 1947, in a 3-2 win over Hungary, and in total he played three times for his country.

The midfielders

Ezio Loik, the engine

Ezio Loik, whose nickname was *Elefante* (the elephant), was born at Fiume, a small town outside Milan, on 26 September 1919. He first made his mark playing for Fiumana before moving to Milan where he was converted to a wing back. His performances for Milan attracted the attention of Venezia to whom he transferred in 1937. At Venezia, Loik met up with another young wing-half of immense talent and a player to whom his career would run an uncanny parallel, Valentino Mazzola. After a series of eye catching performances against them, Torino purchased Loik and Mazzola for 1,200,000 lire, beating off competition from Juventus who had offered 800,000 lire for the pair. It proved to be a master stroke on Novo's part as Loik and Mazzola were to live all the adventures of the Grande Torino from the first Scudetto of 1942-43 until the fateful day of Superga.

His debut in Serie A came at the age of 18, for Milan in a 1-1 draw against Liguria on 16 January 1938. By coincidence, his Torino debut on 4 October 1942 took place in Milan at his old stomping ground of the San Siro Stadium in a 1-0 win over old rivals Ambrosiana (Inter). Loik was a prominent member of the Grande Torino, a fact backed up by the impressive statistic of 72 goals in 181 appearances and recognition in the national team for whom he played nine times and scored four goals after making his debut in a 4-0 victory over Croatia on 5 April 1942.

Loik's name cannot be mentioned without undue reference to Mazzola. The two were regarded as a double act and, despite their different characteristics and personalities, combined to a scintillating effect. Loik's game depended on the way Mazzola performed. Although less naturally talented than Mazzola and not possessing the great inventiveness of his teammate, Loik was always to be found at the heart of the game, competing and contributing. Through their contrasting styles the pair complemented each other almost to perfection: Mazzola was the conductor with Loik very much the engine of the side. Unlike Mazzola, whose eye-catching skills endeared him to spectators, Loik was a more modest player who never attempted to cross the borders of limitation, knowing his own strengths better than anyone and maximising them to their full potential. Technically he was a very accomplished player with good ball control and passing ability and although not blessed with the ability to score spectacular goals, his strike rate was high for such a 'team player'. Although his style did not allow him star player status, his contribution to the success of the Grande Torino was enormous. Where other players sometimes flirted with consistency, Loik, in his own way, was always at the top of his game, sticking to his role with discipline and resilience. Loik always had time to look up before making his pass, his positive and strong mind allowing him to release the ball without any hint of indecision, like an engine always in motion.

Giuseppe 'Pino' Grezar, the power

Giuseppe Grezar was born at Trieste on 25 November 1918. In a midfield role he played for Ampelea and then with Triestina where he made his Serie A debut against Novara (2-0) on 17 September 1939. Novo bought Grezar from Triestina as a contemporary to Loik and Mazzola, his debut for Torino coming on 4 October 1942 in the match against Ambrosiana (1-0). Like his teammate, Menti, he was by nature a quiet person and preferred to express himself on the pitch. Although a reserved and modest character, as a player he was very strong and solid and stood pillar-like in the Torino midfield.

He was less powerful than Mazzola and less courageous than Loik but was nonetheless a dynamic player. There was nothing spectacular about his game; he had a good football mind and was blessed with an ability to do the simple things almost to perfection when others would over-complicate. Subsequently he would never receive the adulation of the fans but his immense contribution was always recognised by those who played with him. A great friend of Aldo Ballarin, the two of them would stick together off the pitch, starting a business together by opening a fabric shop in Turin which unfortunately did not match the success they enjoyed on the pitch. 'Pino', as Grezar was nicknamed, also became a prominent player for the national team and made eight appearances and scored one goal after making his debut at Genoa on 5 April 1942 against Croatia in a 4-0 victory. For Torino, his powerful displays saw 155 appearances and 19 goals.

Eusebio Castigliano, the class

Eusebio Castigliano was born at Vercelli on 9 February 1921. Previously he played for Pro Vercelli, Biellese, Vigevano and Spezia before being bought by Novo in readiness for the 1945-46 season. Like Bacigalupo, Ballarin and Maroso, his debut for Torino came on 14 October 1945 for the Juventus v Torino (2-1) match at the Stadio Comunale. Castigliano was the midfielder with an elegant style all of his own. He was nicknamed *gamba di velluto* (velvet leg) by the supporters due to the elegant manner in which he moved on the pitch. Castigliano's style was reflected in his dress sense and on seeing this very elegant man in 'civilian' clothes it was difficult to believe that he was a footballer. He possessed an athletic physique with a long body adding to his eye-catching appearance on the field. A midfielder of many talents, his ability to dribble with the ball was matched by an equally competitive streak; he was always prepared to fight until the last minute of each game. One of his great strengths as a player was being able to impose himself on the game while also possessing the priceless and uncanny knack of being able to score goals at vital times.

At times as a player he could be arrogant, although in his own way equally generous. During a derby match against Juventus his opposite marker, the Danish player John Hansen, then an idol of the Juventus fans, was unable to dispossess him of the ball. At the end of the match Castigliano picked up the ball and offered it to Hansen, saying that if he wanted the ball, then here it was and that he could now take it home with him and put it underneath his pillow! He also liked to take revenge, often making a mental note of any occasion where scores needed to be settled at a later date. The derby games against Juventus were a prime source of such amusement and in particular the two derby matches of the 1945-46 season. In the first encounter, on 14 October 1945, which also marked his debut for the Granata, Juventus had triumphed 2-1 after Castigliano had gifted them a penalty. Castigliano's pride had taken a bad knock, so it was with great delight when he extracted his revenge in the return match, scoring the only goal when Torino beat Juventus 1-0 at the Stadio Comunale. In total he played 116 matches for Torino, scoring 35 goals. His debut for the national team came on 11 November 1945 in the Switzerland-Italy fixture (4-4) and he played a total of seven matches, scoring one goal. At the end of 1948-49, Castigliano was due to join Inter before fate ensured that his memory remained etched in the burgundy of Torino.

Danilo Martelli, the bonus

Danilo Martelli was born at Castellucchio, a town close to Mantova, on 27 May 1923. He could fill the role of wing-half or midfielder and previous to Torino he played for Marzotto and Brescia where he made his Serie A debut in a goalless draw at Atalanta on 14 October 1945. When Martelli joined Torino during the 1946-47 season he was a university student studying to become a doctor, but he soon became immersed in the Torino club and made his debut in the derby against Juventus on 20 October 1946, the match ending in a goalless draw. He became firm friends with Rigamonti and Bacigalupo, forming the popular 'trio Nizza' as the friends were known.

Although he had been purchased primarily as a squad player, the coaching staff were quick to realise Martelli's versatility and showed no hesitation in considering him for the roles of full-back, wing-half or midfielder. He accepted being cast as a reserve player and was happy to appear in any position in the first team, often joking with his teammates that he would even consider replacing his friend Bacigalupo as goalkeeper if it meant getting a game. Besides his modesty, his versatility made him an invaluable member of the squad and, added to his pleasant personality, these were characteristics that allowed him to overcome what to him were minor disappointments encountered in his career. The hardest moment in his Torino days came during the summer of 1947 when Novo, under pressure to improve the finances of the club, considered selling him, with three teams – Roma, Inter and Alessandria – all keen to gain his services. Novo had already taken the decision to offload him to one of the interested parties when Rigamonti and Bacigalupo knocked at the door of his office to try to persuade him against selling their great friend. Together with the rest of the team they offered to take a cut in wages so that Martelli could stay in the squad. Their appeal could have foundered if it was not for an offer from Livorno who made a request to buy the attacker Guido Tieghi, who had joined the club the previous year. Novo entered into negotiations which resulted in Tieghi being transferred and Martelli remaining at the club. Everyone in the squad was delighted that Martelli was to remain with the Granata, apart from Castigliano who had become a good friend of Tieghi's and shared the same passion for life along with a liking for extravagant ties.

In the following seasons Martelli showed that he deserved to stay in the squad. Despite being considered mainly a squad player he made 72 appearances for Torino and scored ten goals. He also played once for the Italian Under-21 team, in a goalless draw against Croatia on 6 January 1943.

The wingers

Franco Ossola, a new star is discovered

Among the people who helped to shape the formation of the Grande Torino was Antonio Janni. One of his most important discoveries was the exciting talent of Franco Ossola. While coach of the Varese team, Janni would invariably take advantage of breaks between training sessions to retire to a nearby cafe, taking time to contemplate on football matters while at the same time allowing himself some precious moments of relaxation. One such afternoon, he noticed a group of young boys playing football in a large square situated opposite the cafe. Among the group of street urchins one youngster immediately stood out, his elegant control and passing making it appear as though the ball was attached to his feet. It was the young Franco Ossola. From that moment Janni knew that the young boy was born to be a champion.

Born in Varese on 23 August 1921, Ossola made an instant impression on his debut for his hometown team, receiving a standing ovation. It was clear from the first moment that Ossola was destined for greater fame and glories. Torino were quick to recognise his talent, beating off competition from Inter before eventually securing his services for the modest price of 55,000 lire. During the 1939-40 season Ossola made four appearances in the Torino first team, making his debut in a 1-0 victory at Novara on 4 February 1940. The following season, 1940-41 he established himself as an important player, proving equally adept at scoring as well as creating opportunities for his teammates and finishing the season with 15 goals to his credit. Although primarily a winger, Ossola managed a high scoring ratio throughout his Torino career with 86 goals in 176 appearances. He could use both feet and possessed fine ball control and a powerful shot.

A fine sportsman and ambassador for the game, Ossola demonstrated his genial side on the occasion of Torino's monumental 7-0 victory over Roma in April 1946. The match, which effectively marked the arrival of the Grande Torino as the new force in Italian football, was won after an incredible opening 19 minutes had seen Torino register six goals against their shell-shocked opponents. During the half-time interval Piero Ferraris made a suggestion to Mazzola and the rest of the team to stop scoring any further goals to avoid a total humiliation of the Roma club. Mazzola agreed to the idea, reckoning that as the game was already won they could save their energies for future matches. However, as soon as the second half got under way Grezar scored a seventh goal from a free-kick, turning his head away from his teammates as if to apologise for having scored. Moments later Ossola was felled in the penalty box by the Roma striker Andreoli. The Bologna-born referee, Scorzoni, immediately awarded a penalty but before the referee could finalise his decision Ossola picked himself up off the ground and moved the ball a few yards away saying to the referee that he had made a mistake and the offence had been committed outside the penalty area. The referee duly agreed and gave a free-kick instead, sparing further embarrassment to the Roma team and ensuring the final scoreline remained 7-0.

Romeo Menti, the gas

Romeo Menti, the right wing of the Grande Torino, was born at Vicenza on 5 September 1919. His previous clubs were Vicenza, Milan and Fiorentina for whom he made his debut in Serie A against Genoa in a 1-1 draw on 17 September 1939. Torino bought Menti from Fiorentina in 1941 and he played his first match in the Granata colours on 26 October 1941 in a 3-2 home win over Liguria. In 1943, Menti returned to play for Milan and Fiorentina before rejoining Torino for the 1946-47 season. He was a very different player to his left wing counterpart Ossola, relying on an abundance of energy and pace which enabled him to leave opponents trailing in his wake. Menti was a classic player, and he played on the wing with a technique that was rare to see. His game plan was based on simplicity, his pace enabling him to go past defenders almost at will, while the use of both feet allowed him the skill of being able to calculate the most favourable space in which to play the ball. He was a real threat to the opposition, with pace and tenacity coupled with an unorthodox but effective dribbling ability.

Menti's pace was matched by a sharpness of mind, possessing a bright football brain and also a deadly kick. He invented an action that he called *Tiro alla Meo* (Meo's kick), after his nickname 'Meo' by which he was known by the Filadelfia fans. As a dead-ball specialist all the penalties and free-kicks were passed to him. When he prepared to take the kicks Menti would place the ball in a way as if he were caressing it, turning his face to the fans at the Filadelfia and giving a little salute to the opposing goalkeeper before affording a final look to his teammates as if to say, "Don't worry, I'll do it this time."

Menti was a quiet man, his manner being reflected on the pitch where he never found it necessary to protest against decisions or to scorn his teammates. Taking into account the violent treatment sometimes handed out by opposition defenders, his temperament was even more remarkable. Even when on a particular occasion an adversary pushed him into the concrete perimeter wall surrounding the pitch at the Filadelfia 'Meo' kept his cool, preferring to let his superior abilities as a footballer do the talking for him. In private Romeo Menti was a caring, family man who found it difficult to leave Florence for Turin as it meant living apart from his wife and children. Living in another city also meant getting used to a new environment and Menti did not welcome the idea of travelling between the regions of Piedmont and Tuscany during his free time. Although his domestic arrangements were not to his liking, he at least found his footballing home in Turin. With the Granata he played 133 matches and scored 53 goals, winning four Scudettos, his performances being enough to earn recognition in the national team for whom he made seven appearances and scored five goals.

The Centre-Forward

Guglielmo Gabetto, the baron

Gabetto, whose nicknamed was *Il Barone* (the baron), was born in Turin on 24 February 1916. He was a centre-forward and before Torino he had played for Juventus, making his Serie A debut in the black and white stripes on 27 January 1935 against Pro-Vercelli. Gabetto had played in seven championships for Juventus, scoring 86 goals in 164 appearances, so when the news came in the summer of 1941 that Juventus were prepared to release him, it naturally came as a bitter disappointment. Initially he thought it was a signal to end his career but the 330,000 lire spent by Ferruccio Novo in beating off competition from Genoa proved to be an inspirational move on Novo's part as with Torino, Gabetto's career was rejuvenated and he became one of the prominent players of the Grande Torino.

He was technically very gifted and had an exceptional football brain, always being able to anticipate openings for himself and his teammates. He was always scoring goals, and was especially famed for his ability to score in the most complicated fashion, his motto being 'If it is not difficult, I am not interested in scoring'. The majority of Gabetto's goals were deemed 'impossible' goals and to the Granata fans, who adored him, each goal was seen as a little miracle. During the 1930s and 1940s Gabetto took to wearing his jersey outside his shorts, making his tall frame appear even more athletic and making himself an instantly recognisable figure on the field. In his career with Torino from 1941-49, Gabetto scored 125 goals in 225 appearances, forming a formidable duo with Franco Ossola in the process. He made his Torino debut on 2 November 1941 in a 4-1 defeat at Lazio, with his debut for the national team coming in the 4-0 win over Croatia on 5 April 1942, an occasion he marked with a goal, one of five scored in six international appearances.

Ready and waiting – the reserves

Along with the star players who were forging the burgeoning status of the Grande Torino there were, of course, the reserve or squad players. Their mention warrants equal importance in the overall picture as they were the players on whom the future Torino sides of the 1950s were to be based, once Mazzola and company had departed.

Pietro 'Pierino' Operto

Born in Turin on 20 December 1926, Pietro Operto was a talented full-back who played for the Piedmont and Casale team prior to being purchased by Torino in the summer of 1948. He was discovered by a Torino scout who saw him as the natural heir to Virgilio Maroso. Operto was playing for Casale together with his brother and, as a Turin man born and bred, could not believe his good fortune when a director of the Casale club told him that Torino were interested in buying him. The transfer proved easy with Novo agreeing a salary of 63,000 lire per month with the defender and a fee of 5,000,000 lire to Casale. He made his debut for Torino in Serie A in a 4-0 home win against Roma on 30 October 1948 and went on to play 11 matches in the 1948-49 season. Operto was a highly promising talent with good technical skills for a full-back but was sadly never allowed the time to prove himself.

Dino Ballarin

Dino was the younger brother of Aldo, and was also born at Chioggia, (close to Venice) on 11 December 1925. Torino purchased him direct from his hometown team Chioggia, to be the third-choice goalkeeper behind Bacigalupo and Gandolfi. With the consistency of the other two goalkeepers, Ballarin never officially made an appearance for Torino and the opportunity to play in Serie A was sadly denied him by time.

Rubens Fadini

One of nine brothers, Rubens Fadini was born at Jolanda di Savoia, close to the city of Ferrara, on 1 June 1927. He was a midfielder and wing-half and previously played for

Cerretti and Tanfani and the Gallaratese club in Serie B. Although there were several clubs keen to secure his services, Torino headed the queue and Fadini was transferred from Gallaratese in the summer of 1948, initially as cover for Grezar and Castigliano. His debut for Torino in Serie A came on 7 November 1948, in a 1-0 win against Lazio, displaying the talent that had both Ferruccio Novo and Leslie Lievesley believing that in him they had found a new Torino champion for the next decade of the 1950s. Fadini was a young player who already possessed the type of temperament and character that had him earmarked as a future champion and, along with his undoubted skill and movement, he was a great header of the ball. His potential knew no bounds but he played in only ten matches for the Grande Torino in 1948-49.

Julius Schubert

The midfielder Julius Schubert was born in Budapest, Hungary on 12 December 1922. After the war he emigrated to Czechoslovakia where he obtained a Czech passport and eventually became a player in the national team. He was spotted playing for AK Bratislava by Egri Erbstein, who immediately wanted to bring him to Torino. However, his transfer to Torino was a rather drawn-out and complex affair, with the Czech club naturally none too keen to lose their best player. The ploy of Schubert not to turn up for Bratislava soon convinced the club of their decision to sell him to Torino and once more Novo was able to get his man.

Schubert was another highly talented footballer and played his first and only season for Torino in 1948-49, making his debut in Serie A in the 2-2 draw at Palermo on 6 January 1949, deputising in Mazzola's role for five matches and scoring one goal against Pro Patria with an amazing free-kick. Although unable to speak a word of Italian, he soon struck up a good friendship with Eusebio Castigliano. Just a few days before scoring his first goal for Torino, Castigliano took him on a tour of the city, stopping on the way at the Cafe Torino in Piazza San Carlo where he instructed Schubert to perform a gesture which none of the Torino players had done before. Castigliano told his new-found friend to rub the sole of his shoes above the rampant bull engraved on the walking path outside the entry to the cafe. Schubert followed his friend's instructions and the magic spell worked when on the following Sunday he scored his goal.

Ruggero Grava

Born at Claut near Udine on 26 April 1922, Ruggero Grava could play as a winger or centre-forward and was earmarked by the coaching staff as a possible successor to Gabetto. He played in France for Roubaix where he won a championship in 1947 before signing for Torino, making a solitary appearance in a 3-0 defeat at Genoa on 26 January 1948. His ability was never in doubt but, like the other squad players, was cruelly denied the chance to prove it.

Emile Bongiorni

The Frenchman Emile Bongiorni was born at Boulogne Billancourte, France, on 19 March 1921. After the war he played as a centre-forward for the Racing Club de Paris where he proved to be a popular performer, winning five international caps for France. Although not the tallest of players he had a strong physique, excellent dribbling skills and a powerful shot. When he joined Torino in the summer of 1948 at the age of 27 he brought with him excellent credentials and was viewed by Novo as an investment for the future and the long term replacement for Gabetto. Bongiorni was a great all-round attacking player, though, and Lievesley soon recognised his ability, wanting to transform him into an attacking wing-half with the job of supporting Grava. The opportunity was never to materialise and Bongiorni made only eight appearances and scored two goals for Torino after making his Serie A debut in a goalless draw at Fiorentina on 19 December 1948.

Valerio Bacigalupo.

Aldo Ballarin.

Virgilio Maroso.

Sauro Toma.

Mario Rigamonti.

Ezio Loik.

Giuseppe Grezar.

Eusebio Castigliar

Danilo Martelli.

Franco Ossola.

Romeo Menti.

Guglielmo Gabetto.

Pietro Operto.

Dino Ballarin.

Rubens Fadini.

Julius Schubert.

Ruggero Grava.

Emile Bongiorni

The Talisman –
Valentino Mazzola

O N 31 May 1942, with three matches remaining to the end of the championship season, Torino visited Venezia still harbouring faint hopes of overtaking the league leaders, Roma. Having beaten their opponents earlier in the season, confidence in the camp was high and going into the fixture on the back of a 9-1 hammering of Atalanta, two points seemed a certainty at the Sant Elena stadium. Tactics went much to plan with Torino taking the lead after only five minutes through a goal from Petron, leaving the watching Ferruccio Novo to feel that victory was assured even at such an early stage of the game. However, the goal merely proved the catalyst for a wave of Venezia attacks with Torino forced to defend deep into their own penalty area before the non-stop pressure eventually led to an equalising goal. Leading the Venezia onslaught were the duo of Ezio Loik and Valentino Mazzola, a highly talented pair of footballers whose understanding of each other appeared to onlookers as though they were practising telepathy.

In the 37th minute Torino conceded a second goal from the penalty spot after Ferrini had handled, but Novo remained undaunted, thinking his side could salvage at least a point; after all, there remained ample time on the clock. Venezia, though, had other ideas and, inspired in midfield by the brilliant promptings of Mazzola and the sheer physical presence of Loik, kept up the incredible tempo and added a third goal. For all their endeavour and spirit, Torino had been unable to impose themselves on a game totally dominated by the duo of Mazzola and Loik.

The mood in the home dressing-room contrasted sharply to the feeling of dejection felt by the away team who had prepared for the verbal volley that Novo would certainly deliver for throwing away what appeared to be their last chance of the Scudetto. Instead, and much to their surprise, Novo headed straight to the home dressing-room to congratulate the Venezia team, and in particular Mazzola and Loik, on their fine performance. Although Novo's gesture was sporting, he had, of course, another agenda in mind, which was quickly recognised by the Juventus scout Rosetta who was also in the changing-room offering his congratulations. Juventus had been tracking the two Venezia players for some months, having failed in an audacious attempt to prise Loik from his previous club, Milan. With Loik and Mazzola now complementing each other's play almost to perfection, Juventus and Rosetta had been forced to reconsider their strategy and were now keen on purchasing both players. Thinking that they were the only interested party, Juventus were in no rush to buy and were prepared to wait until the right opportunity arose. Their patience was encouraged by the knowledge that the management of the Venezia club were willing to cash in on their most valuable assets in order to bring much-needed money into the club. The procrastination of the Juventus club, however, proved fatal and Novo's appearance in the Venezia changing-room made Rosetta and his paymasters realise that the players were now destined for the Filadelfia.

Like numerous other times in his career, Novo had outsmarted his rivals. A deal was soon struck with the Venezia president, Aldo Bennato, who was desperate for funds to improve the financial standing and development of his club. The deal involved Torino paying the sum of 1,200,000 lire plus two players, Petron and Mezzada, in part exchange. Realising it was too good an offer to refuse, Bennato badly underestimated the popularity of the duo with the Venezia fans who were outraged at the impending departure of their two stars. As news of the transfer became public, an angry group of Venezia fans marched to the club's headquarters. To defuse the volatile situation, Bennato was forced to appear at the window of his office and show the fans the cheque Novo had given him, shouting to them that the deal had secured the financial future of the club. The transfer, however, soon raised eyebrows all over Italy, especially among factory workers whose average daily wage was 15 lire. The fee appeared astronomical as it was possible to assemble almost an entire team with the money Torino had paid out for only two players. Novo, though, remained unmoved by the fuss, more convinced than ever that in Loik and especially Mazzola he had found the vital link for his master plan.

The Captain

Valentino Mazzola was born in Cassano D'Adda, a town close to Milan, on 26 January 1919. From an early age it was clear to those around him that his natural talent would lead to a successful career in football. After playing for the minor teams of Tresoldi and the works team of Alfa Romeo in Milan, his abilities were recognised by Venezia and after signing contract terms with them he made his Serie A debut on 31 March 1940 in a 1-0 defeat against Lazio. A series of match-winning performances for the Venezia club, culminating in a brilliant display in the 3-1 win over Torino in May 1942, had convinced Novo that Mazzola was the inspiration he was seeking for the side. In the scheme of Novo's grand opera, Mazzola's role was to conduct the orchestra.

Mazzola had the rare ability of appearing in complete control, proving equally adept in the air as well as when the ball was at his feet. Such traits were rare in players of the period and have remained so to this day, not only in the history of the Italian game but also at world level. Players able to perform the full range of technical skills to a maximum level were an almost complete rarity, but in Mazzola, Torino had unearthed a truly remarkable player. He had an excellent physique and though only 1.7m tall, his enormous thighs enabled him to kick naturally with both feet while also allowing him to perform incredible feats of athleticism such as allegedly being able to jump higher than the crossbar. His adversaries could never work out which was his favoured foot and everyone assumed that as a youngster he had spent countless hours practising the exercise of 'wall kicking'. This consisted of kicking a football against a wall using both feet with the ball rebounding back to the player on both sides. Coupled with a footballing equivalent of a sixth sense, Mazzola could influence the tightest of matches, turning games locked in stalemate into victory. Added to his steely determination it was easy to see why teammates and opponents alike saw him as a class act and a player to be respected.

Equally enthusiastic at the signing of the new wing-half were the Torino supporters, who immediately warmed to their new player, quickly recognising that the club had in their ranks a rare talent capable of inspiring the team to greater things still. Mazzola immediately became Torino's standard bearer, commanding the total respect of his teammates by his undoubted football ability as well as his strong leadership qualities which made him the obvious choice as captain. His ability to extract greater commitment from his teammates was appreciated by the fans at the Filadelfia who were never slow in showing their discontent during games when the team was not winning. On such occasions, the sound of a bugle would signal to Mazzola and his teammates the need for greater commitment. One fan in particular, named Bolmida, became a well-known figure at Torino for his impromptu musical renderings. On hearing the shrills of Bolmida's bugle, Mazzola would invariably pull up his shirt sleeves as a signal to the trio of Loik, Castigliano and Grezar to demand more effort from the rest of the team. The gesture would also prompt Mazzola to set off in pursuit of the ball, demanding it from his teammates at every opportunity.

Mazzola would begin a 'match within a match', showing off his sublime skill to great effect, although never to the detriment of his teammates who were only too willing to take directions from the master. It also indicated that point in the match when Torino stepped up their performance, snatching many vital victories. During the glory years of the Grande Torino, the resounding response which Mazzola and his colleagues gave to the fans became a memory to rank alongside any of the famous triumphs.

The private life of Valentino

The success enjoyed by Mazzola the footballer was in direct contrast to his private life where he was misunderstood by many of the people closest to him. By marrying twice, an unusual occurrence in the Italy of the 1940s, he had already captured unwarranted public attention. His first marriage, to Emilia in 1946, had produced the two sons, Sandro and Ferruccio, but the couple constantly rowed and separation soon became inevitable, although with no divorce law existing in Italy he was forced to obtain the cancellation of the marriage in Romania. With the marriage dissolved, Mazzola was free to wed his new lady friend, Giuseppina Cutrone, in a ceremony which took place in Vienna.

Although wreathed in star quality each time he stepped on to a football pitch, Mazzola was an altogether quieter man away from the matchday glare, preferring simpler entertainment – such as eating in good restaurants and playing bowls – to the glitzier type of nightlife enjoyed by some of his teammates. Essentially he was of a different composition and loved nothing more than taking his young son, Sandro, to the Filadelfia, although at home he would speak little about his job or the club. The charismatic figure which he cut on the field was not mirrored in his social life where, without a football to inspire him, his presence remained that of a mere mortal compared to the god-like status afforded to him as a footballer. Despite not possessing the same powers off the field, Mazzola remained an immensely popular figure among his teammates and the press who bestowed on him the slogan 'Il Torino + Mazzola', meaning that the team was made greater by his genius. The unique appeal of the Torino captain was not slow to be recognised by those around him and upon his return from the club's successful tour of Brazil in 1948, a deal was struck to lend his name to a particular manufacturer's football boots. This early form of player sponsorship highlighted the massive marketing potential of Mazzola's name, with the player himself equally keen on exploiting his football fame to the full.

Like father like son

Despite the increasing glare of publicity, to which he grew accustomed, Mazzola took great joy in taking his little son, Sandro, along to training sessions at the Filadelfia with the young boy, then six years old, looking on in awe as his father went about his rigorous training schedules. To the eyes of his young son, Mazzola appeared like a giant although at the time Sandro had no idea what his father meant to the club and would learn this later from friends, family and supporters. The little boy scurrying around the training pitch was simply imitating his father whom he loved dearly. Apart from his father, another figure at the training ground who created a lasting impression on the young Sandro was the caretaker of the stadium, an old man called Zoso, who took time out to look after his little training boots and even assign him a place in the locker room. Sandro strongly believed that he, too, would one day play for Torino but to his great disappointment the club ignored him during his youth and he joined Inter instead. Years after watching his father in training, Sandro Mazzola returned to the Filadelfia as part of the Inter youth team for a fixture against Torino but the only person to remember him was the old caretaker, Zoso. Being the son of the famous Valentino created more curiosity than envy and Sandro went on to enjoy a great career himself with Inter and the national team, becoming, like his father, one of the most famous players in Italian football, although he never forgot the way Torino turned their back on him.

The first flight

Besides his many attributes, Valentino Mazzola was a man of great emotion who recorded his thoughts in writing, often keeping a diary when he became overwhelmed by special events. One such occurrence was during his first flight on, 5 July 1946, when Torino flew south to play Bari in the final stage of the championship.

Mazzola wrote: *On boarding the plane we had our photograph taken and after taking our seats inside we took off. The first to feel sick is Loik, the fittest member of the squad. He laid his head on Piacentini's shoulder and looked at me with a very pale expression. I looked around to see Gabetto and Grezar playing cards. I found my first flight to be rather pleasant. I have always had the desire to fly and this desire has always helped to keep any bad thoughts away from my mind. At about 2,000 metres high it is quite cold so we re-wear the coats that we had taken off when we left. Everything is ok, underneath us are the mountains of the region of Liguria and we have just flown over Genoa, getting close to La Spezia. Loik has gone to the pilot's cabin. The atmosphere on the plane is very calm, everyone is smiling now and the fear of flying that troubled everyone has gone. After an hour of flight we are over La Spezia, the views are fantastic, everyone is looking out of their windows! Loik has returned, he is so funny he is completely covered by his overcoat! Now we are flying over Florence, some of us are feeling hungry but our destination is still far away. I am developing a headache, I knew it would happen as when I was a sailor on the ship I never felt sea-sick, only headaches. We are just over one hour away from Bari, and Cortina offers me a glass of Grappa with mint which makes me feel much better. We are now passing over a white cloud and I cannot see anything else from my little window, we are now 3,000 metres high and everything is white and very cold. Loik is still feeling unwell, the President is now waking up and has noticed that his coat is covering my legs. He has just told me that I owe him 800 lire for the dry cleaning! We are close to Bari, now, I am just curious to know how the landing will be. We are getting really low now, and above the air field the landing has been carried out magnificently. Now we are getting off, all of us happy after 3 hours and 30 minutes of flight.*

Mazzola and fascism

Three days after securing a 1-0 victory in the derby against Juventus, on 16 March 1947, a full Torino team, led by Mazzola, undertook a friendly fixture against the Casale club at their small Natale Palli ground. The match was billed as a charity event with all profits going to the families of the partisans who had died in the war. As expected, Torino won a comfortable match 4-1, raising 180,000 lire, although more money would have been collected if the weather on the day been kinder as strong wind and heavy rain prevented many spectators from attending. The match helped to answer certain allegations of the supposed link between the Torino club and the Fascists, although no such claim had ever been proved. However, some rumours had abounded during the war and a group of partisans even thought of kidnapping the Torino squad at a friendly match. The plan was abandoned at the last minute.

None of the Torino players, including Mazzola, had in public shown personal allegiance or political tendencies to the fascist regime. As footballers, they had the privilege of earning good money and enjoying more freedom than their fellow countrymen, so in certain ways they appeared to adapt to the political climate which had engulfed Italy during the war years. Due to his various business interests Ferruccio Novo was obliged to adhere to the fascist regime and did not hide a certain curiosity in fascism, although he kept his interest strictly private. However, Novo's fascist leanings have to be measured against the lengths he had gone to in helping protect his colleague, Egri Erbstein, who, being a Jew, was persecuted by the racial law. Thanks to Novo's support, Erbstein was able to return to the Torino club once the war ended. Despite the rumours, no evidence existed that the club had collaborated with the Fascists. Due to the geographical distance between Turin and the capital, Rome, the regime was not imposed with the same strictness that surrounded the central and southern parts of the country. Italian fascism was centred in Rome with its main propaganda targets being the Lazio and Roma clubs, a fact highlighted by Roma's championship success in 1941-42 which was well received by the authorities.

The way they were

The Grande Torino of Mazzola created a great deal of interest throughout Italy, but during that period the guise of the celebrity did not exist and the life of a football player was still lived around those of the ordinary working class people. Mazzola proved no exception to the rule, despite his star status, and was never arrogant or aloof, remaining close to the people who came to watch him play. It was not uncommon for footballers to carry out tedious tasks around their club. On more than one occasion during winter, the players would arrive for training and find the Filadelfia pitch covered in deep snow which fell from the nearby Alps. To allow them to train, Mazzola and his teammates thought nothing of arming themselves with shovels and clearing the snow from the pitch. The gesture was reciprocated by the supporters on match days when an army of volunteers would clear the pitch to ensure the game went ahead.

Wherever Mazzola and his teammates travelled, they would attract enormous crowds and on one occasion, at the city of Palermo in Sicily, the police were obliged to protect the hotel where the players were staying to avoid an intrusion from a party of enthusiastic fans. Such was their popularity that even the Mafia boss, Giuliano, sent a message of goodwill to the team. The glory which surrounded Mazzola and his squad did not lead to any kind of goldfish bowl existence and for away matches they travelled by train, or by their famed mini bus, named the Conte Rosso, always with a large number of loyal fans in tow. For the away fixture at Alessandria in January 1947, the players travelled by rail from Turin accompanied by hundreds of supporters who packed every wagon of the train. The entire duration of the journey was spent in conversation between players and supporters, with Mazzola being the focal point of the fans' attention. On another occasion the team had experienced severe problems when setting out for a fixture in the region of Liguria on board the Conte Rosso. Motorways were not yet in existence and the bus had to travel along B roads. When the bus arrived in the Alps it encountered a heavy snowstorm which resulted in the engine failing, leaving the bus and its passengers stranded. Leading by example, as he always did on the pitch, Mazzola encouraged the other players to get off the bus and dig the snow from the vehicle so they could continue on their journey.

The friendship enjoyed between the Torino team and supporters was also extended to opposition players and on match days it was common for Mazzola and his teammates to share a meal with their opponents at Il Cervo restaurant in Turin just a few hours prior to kick-off. They would eat together as friends, although no quarter would be given when they met later on the pitch. After matches, Mazzola and some of the other players frequented the bar Fiorio in the city centre of Turin, to listen to the radio and talk with supporters before sometimes moving on to the bar Vittoria, owned by Gabetto and Ossola who enjoyed serving drinks to the players while working behind the bar.

A man in demand

As one of the best talents in the world football, Mazzola was the player that all Italian footballers wished to play alongside. The Torino players recognised this and were happy to ask Novo to pay him double the salaries they were earning in view of all the success he had helped bring to the club. However, Mazzola was considering leaving Torino and had learned that Inter were prepared to offer him a package that would be difficult to turn down and which would mean financial security for him and his family. Mazzola tried speaking to Novo about his need for a new challenge in his career, but the president avoided any discussion on the matter, knowing perfectly well that if he allowed Mazzola to join Inter he would effectively be handing them the Scudetto. Mazzola was hurt by what he saw as a rejection on Novo's part and confided his feelings in a letter written in September 1948 to a journalist friend, Nino Oppio.

Dear Nino,

Although it is my wish to join Inter it will not be possible. The directors of Torino would prefer see me ruined rather that playing for Inter. Is it possible that in a democratic era as we are living, I cannot have the freedom to choose between Inter and Torino? Torino do not want to give me away to reinforce Inter. At Torino I get 2,500,000 lire while Inter will offer me 10,000,000 lire! Don't you think it is in my interest to join Inter? Torino want champion after champion but they are not interested in paying this amount! Because of such egotism from Torino do I have to lose millions? Inter at the moment need players who can dominate to please their fans who have become very angry.

Mazzola planned further talks with Novo at the end of the 1948-49 season to try to persuade him of the need for a new challenge in his career. Novo had always envisaged Mazzola finishing his playing days with Torino and fate ultimately agreed with him.

Valentino
Mazzola in
action.

Valentino
Mazzola.

Mazzola (left) alongside his great
mentor Ferruccio Novo.

Like father like son.
Mazzola tying up
the bootlaces of the
young Sandro at
the Filadelfia
Stadium.

The captain
Mazzola
leading Torino
out at
snowbound
Bari, 22
February 1948.

The Adventure of Il Grande Torino

The first Scudetto of Il Grande Torino 1942-43

THE team that became known throughout Italy as Il Grande Torino first stepped into football immortality in 1942-43. After several years of consolidation the squad was augmented by several key signings and the campaign was to mark the first of five consecutive championships. In the previous season Torino had used the WM system with a great degree of success when finishing as runners-up to Roma. However the system was temporarily abandoned for the opening two matches which both ended in defeat. The third game of the season, on 18 October 1942, pitched Torino against their great rivals Juventus at the Stadio Comunale. With defeat something which could not be contemplated, Ferruccio Novo decided the team should revert to the WM system with the midfield of Baldi, new arrival Grezar and the duo of Loik and Mazzola supplementing the attack of Menti, Ferraris and Gabetto. The result was an astounding 5-2 victory, with goals from Menti (2), Loik, Mazzola and Ferraris launching the season in memorable fashion. The momentum of the derby win then carried over into a fine run which included victories at home over Genoa 3-1, Fiorentina 5-0, Triestina 4-1 and away against Roma 4-0 and Venezia 3-0.

The surprise team of the season was proving to be the emerging Livorno, who after eight matches already held a five-point advantage at the top of the table. Their surge to the top included a 2-1 win against Torino at the Filadelfia in the second match of the season when Torino had used the method system. Although a first-half goal from Loik put Torino in control, Livorno hit back with second-half goals from Zidarish and Degano to claim the points. The tightly contested match had signalled that the race for the championship would be a competitive one.

The fine winning run that Torino put together was ended by Milan who triumphed 1-0 at the Filadelfia on 22 November. However, this proved only a minor set-back as three successive victories followed, allowing Torino to draw level at the top with Livorno. Going into 1943, the team was well placed to continue its assault on the championship but a 3-1 home defeat by Ambrosiana in January, and a goalless draw at rivals Livorno, meant that some ground had been lost. The team's inconsistency was proving infuriating with the finger of blame being pointed in the direction of the coach, Andrea Kutik. Although renowned as a good technical coach, Kutik had a liking for the good life and in particular fine wine, a habit which at times appeared to cloud his thinking and affect his job. He was a frequent customer of the Tre Galline restaurant and would actively encourage the players to share his love of the good life. Novo soon reacted to what he considered to be a bad influence on the players and replaced Kutik with Antonio Janni. The decision was inevitable because in Italy it was commonly accepted that alcohol and football did not mix. Janni was more single-minded in his approach to the game and Novo reckoned on his strict discipline and fanatical commitment to the cause spreading throughout the squad.

Earlier in the season the WM system had been reintroduced for the derby against Juventus who, as a strange coincidence, were the next opponents after the coaching reshuffle. This time Torino beat their rivals 2-0 at the Filadelfia to complete the double. Just as before, the derby victory boosted the team's morale and following a thrilling 3-3 draw against Genoa they thrashed the reigning champions, Roma, 4-0 before clinching a 3-2 win at Fiorentina. At the same time Livorno kept on winning and when Torino slipped up again against Milan at the San Siro on 7 March, it meant Livorno held a four-point lead.

From that moment, however, Torino did not look back, winning their remaining seven matches inspired by the brilliance of Valentino Mazzola. As the season drew to its conclusion, Torino and Livorno were locked together at the top of the table. The key moment came on 4 April, the 27th week of the season, when Torino beat Atalanta 4-2 while Livorno were defeated by Roma. Torino now held a single-point lead with the positions remaining unchanged as the teams entered the last game of the season. On Easter Day, 25 April 1943, Livorno entertained Milan who were in mid-table, while Torino faced an away match at Bari who needed at least a point to avoid relegation to Serie B. While Livorno won an easy game, Torino were forced to fight out a highly competitive match against a desperate Bari side. With only three minutes remaining, a goalless scoreline meant the likelihood of a play-off match between the two sides. Then Mazzola again provided the inspiration with a late goal to clinch the Scudetto for Torino. Amid wild scenes of celebration the Grande Torino of Ferruccio Novo were Campione d'Italia for the first time.

A bitter end for Roma but a sweet double for Torino

The joy of winning the championship soon turned into a double celebration with triumph in the Coppa Italia. And with this dual success Torino became the first side in Italian football to win both trophies in the same season, a remarkable feat achieved in a landmark campaign. The cup competition, consisting of 34 teams, had started earlier in the season. Although not regarded as prestigious as the Scudetto, the Coppa Italia offered another chance of silverware, an opportunity too good to be passed up. After an easy 7-0 win against Anconitana on 20 September, Torino progressed to the next round seven days later with a 2-0 success over Atalanta in Bergamo. The final matches were contested after the league championship had been settled in April and in the third round Torino thrashed a Milan side, led by the centre-forward Boffi, one of the best players of the last decade, 5-0 at the Filadelfia. Destiny then saw Torino, the new emerging side, confront one of the great teams of recent years, Roma, in the semi-final. Prior to the match at the Filadelfia, a strange occurrence took place. A young Torino supporter delivered a small parcel and bunch of flowers to the Turin hotel where the Roma team were staying, with the request that the parcel be passed to their club officials. On opening the mysterious package the Roma directors found a pair of scissors inside, and a message written on the ticket attached to the flowers which read: 'Welcome to Turin, but cut off the Scudetto from your shirts'. The message referred to the decision, made a month earlier by Roma, to exercise their rights, as the reigning champions, to keep the tricolour Scudetto patch on their shirts. Although the Federation had proclaimed Torino as the new league champions, Roma had insisted on keeping the patch until their right 'expired' on 30 June. Torino officials were incensed by the decision, with their supporters keen on venting their anger towards the Roma club. On the day of the match, 23 May 1943, the Roma team met with a crescendo of whistles and insults as they took the field in the most volatile of atmospheres.

The match itself was a scrappy affair littered with fouls. In the second half the game exploded after a strike from the Roma forward Dagianti cancelled out a goal from Loik which had put Torino in front. With about 15 minutes remaining, a free-kick from Ferraris was blocked by the hand of Brunella, the Roma right-back, but despite the appeals of the Torino players the Florence referee Pizziolo did not give a penalty. A few minutes later a shot from Ossola was saved by the Roma goalkeeper Blason on the goal line but the referee, perhaps atoning for his earlier mistake, ruled that the ball had crossed the line and awarded a goal to Torino. The controversial decision angered the Roma supporters to such an extent that a group of them rushed on to the pitch, jostling the referee in an attempt to get the decision reversed. In the confusion the game carried on and Ossola added a third goal after running through the stationary Roma defence who were busy disputing with the referee who had by now totally lost control. Blason demonstrated his contempt at the decision and added to the ensuing shambles with his own show of petulance, throwing every football out of the stadium until there were none left to carry on the game. Referee Pizziolo had by this stage had enough and with five minutes still on the clock blew the final whistle to end the game.

After the match there was much controversy, and recriminations from all sides including an abortive demand for the match to be replayed. The 3-1 result was eventually declared void and the decision was given to award the match 2-0 to Torino. In the most controversial fashion Torino had reached the Cup Final and the chance to create history. Standing in the way of the double were Venezia, who included in their line-up the former Torino player, Petron. The match was played at the neutral venue of the San Siro in Milan on 30 May 1943. After the drama of the semi-final, Torino recorded a comfortable 4-0 win with goals from Ossola (2), Mazzola and Ferraris. The tricolour badge and Scudetto shield were now firmly embroidered on the Granata shirts.

Torino-Fiat and the championship during World War Two, 1944

Torino's satisfaction at their success of a league and cup double was immense but the triumph was soon overshadowed by greater events still. On the same day that the championship was won, 25 April 1943, Allied troops disembarked in Sicily and the war came home to every Italian. Many cities had already been ravaged by air-raids and a bomb had even destroyed a staircase at the Filadelfia, but incredibly the game of football carried on. The signing of an armistice on 8 September 1943 had divided Italy into two parts, the north and the south, and with the constant dangers presented by the war, football naturally had to adapt. The Serie A championship was suspended due to the ever-present threat of air-raids making it difficult for teams to move around the country to play away matches. Football was now played only at a regional level, although even then not every region in Italy could afford to participate.

A new war tournament, the Alta Italia 1944, split into three rounds, started with teams of varied levels taking part. The tournament was divided into six groups: Piemontese-Ligure, Lombardo, Veneto, Giuliano, Misto, Emiliano-Toscano. Each group consisted of a number of teams with the region of Piemontese-Ligure comprising Torino, Juventus, Biellese, Liguria, Genoa, Novara, Asti, Casale, Alessandria and Cuneo. This was no Scudetto, of course. The tournament was a wartime distraction, devised to keep the game going in some form ready for the eventual resumption of Serie A. Because of the war some clubs had to move from their cities of origin, and some were forced to change their names to reflect the companies whose employment kept their players from the army. Torino became known as Torino-Fiat due to the persistence of Ferruccio Novo, who kept the team together by playing under the guise of the works side of the Fiat firm where the players held work permits. Juventus had moved to the city of Alba, situated outside Turin, which was the home of the Cisitalia car company owned by Signor Dusio, the president of Juventus.

The north of Italy was organised into the Piedmont-Liguria championship which, at the semi-final stage, joined with the region of Lombardia. The tournament had no set fixture list because continual aerial bombardment meant that it was impossible to set dates or even locations. Most of the teams' line-ups were weakened because the majority of players had been called up for military service. For this reason the tournament was open to everyone such as in the case of Silvio Piola, the centre-forward of Lazio. Piola had returned to his hometown of Vercelli, situated close to Turin, to collect his family to take them to Rome. However, after the armistice it was increasingly difficult to leave the north and on 8 September 1943 he found himself stranded in Piedmont. It was just too dangerous to travel to Rome. Prevented from playing for Lazio, Piola had little choice but to settle in the north. When Novo heard of Piola's predicament he had no hesitation in offering him employment with Torino who were in need of star players. Piola immediately accepted the offer, partly because he welcomed the opportunity of playing alongside Loik and Mazzola.

Vittorio Pozzo had also recommended that all members of the Italian national side should move to Piedmont to be closer to him. Piola soon learned that fellow international stars were also keen on joining Torino, with the Fiorentina goalkeeper Griffanti being the next player to sign for the Torino-Fiat club. Some of the Torino players who had won the Scudetto the previous season had moved in the opposite direction, however, with Giuseppe Grezar playing for the Ampelea isle of Istria for the region of Venezia-Giulia, and Romeo Menti joining Milan for the region of Lombardia.

Having been forced to move from the Filadelfia, Torino played their home matches at the Velodromo site in the city. Due to the low standard of some of the teams in the championship – such as Cuneo and Asti – the Torino-Fiat side were able to play more relaxed football on occasions and topped the regional table with 34 points from 18 matches with 78 goals scored and 19 against. Among the highlights of the early stage of the tournament were big wins against Juventus 5-0, Genoa 7-0, Biellese 7-1, Alessandria 7-0 and Novara 8-2. Although Torino had enjoyed a comfortable passage to the next stage, several players caught the eye of Ferruccio Novo, in particular the Biellese midfielder Eusebio Castigliano, who joined Torino the following season.

The next stage of the tournament, the semi-finals, saw the top two of the Piemontese-Ligure round, Torino and Juventus, matched against the top two teams of the Lombardia region, Ambrosiana and Varese, with the teams playing each other twice to form a mini league. Torino started badly with a 3-1 defeat against Juventus in the first leg. They recovered to beat Varese 2-1 and 6-0 and then Ambrosiana 6-2 before finishing with 3-3 draws against Juventus and Ambrosiana. The sequence of results was enough to put Torino into the Final where they faced Venezia and the *vigili del fuoco* (fire brigade) team of VF Spezia.

A new tactic and an incredible defeat

Despite the increasing hazards of the war, all three teams managed to get to Milan where the Final was to be played. On 16 July 1943, and with tiredness taking its toll, Torino were beaten 2-1 by VF Spezia. It was an incredible result. The Fiat-Torino team, effectively the Grande Torino and the reigning champions of Italy, had been humbled by a team of firemen. The Spezia coach was a former Genoa player called Barbieri, who adopted a revolutionary style of play named the 'half system', which he used to great effect. Barbieri posted one of his defenders to mark the opposing centre-forward and placed another on the shoulder of the marking defender. The covering defender was therefore afforded a free role and was able to cover up any mistakes made by the marker. With this tactic Barbieri anticipated the birth of a new role called the *libero* (more commonly known today as the sweeper) and was able to confuse the strategies of his opposing coach. Against a great team like Torino, though, the tactic alone would not be sufficient, so other factors were needed to produce victory.

In 1944 a number of regional representative games had been organised with one such game taking place on 9 July, at Trieste, between Piedmont and Venezia-Giulia, a match which ended in a 2-2 draw. The Piedmont team normally comprised Torino and Juventus players but for this match the formation consisted of Torino players only as the Juventus team were unwilling to undertake such a long and dangerous journey to the Adriatic port. The Piedmont-Torino squad departed at dawn on the Friday before the match, arriving at Trieste just a couple of hours before kick-off and having endured bad weather on their journey and losing some of their baggage in the process. It was an arduous trip but they desperately wanted to fulfil their obligation to play against Venezia-Giulia. The return journey to Turin was equally as bad and it was an exhausted squad which prepared for the final fixture, against VF Spezia. The Federation recognised this and offered to change the date of the match but Novo refused, taking the view that even a tired Torino side would be good enough to overcome a weaker team like VF Spezia.

Alas, for once Novo's judgement was impaired and his arrogance proved costly. The Spezia team arrived fresh in Milan, finding accommodation in an old convent thanks to the co-operation of some nuns. Taking advantage of their isolation they planned their tactics and enjoyed a full day's rest. Their preparation paid off the following day when they caught Torino off guard with two goals from Angelini before Piola managed a consolation. The shocked Torino team, aided by a few days' rest, then beat Venezia 5-2 but it was VF Spezia who took the championship. As the tournament was unofficial, Spezia's title was never recognised by the Federation. Nevertheless the achievement of Barbieri and his squad was remarkable and proved that in football anything was possible, a fact not lost on Novo and the Torino players; despite only two defeats in 26 matches, and 31 goals from Piola, they had been beaten to the title by a team of firemen.

Peace at last but a violent match

With the war in Europe nearing its end, Allied troops were rapidly taking control in areas previously occupied by the Nazis. The city of Turin was liberated on 25 April 1945, exactly two years to the day since Torino had won the last Scudetto. Just before the liberation a tournament was organised between two Torino teams and two Juventus teams: Torino-Fiat, Filiale-Fiat, Juventus and Cisitalia. Although the tournament was never concluded, a memorable match took place between Torino and Juventus on Easter Day 1945. The game was staged at the Stadio Comunale to commemorate the memory of the former Juventus director and former player Pio Marchi who had died during a bombing raid.

Close to the end of the second half, with Juventus leading 2-1, a strong challenge from the former Torino player Borel, who was now with Juventus, provoked a strong reaction from Mazzola. The challenge so angered the Torino captain that he threw a punch at Borel who was able to avoid the blow, the result being that Mazzola ended up on the ground. The Juventus player Rava immediately rushed to Borel's assistance and a mass brawl erupted involving all the players including the reserves. As the fighting continued, a spectator, possibly a soldier, watching from one of the central standing areas, fired shots into the air. Other spectators, probably in panic, also started shooting. Of course, these were still volatile times with political differences remaining very much intact. Amid the panic, the players fell to the ground as the firing carried on for a couple of minutes. Amazingly, when calm was restored the match resumed, but within minutes the players began fighting again and more shots were fired into the air. The gunfire may have come from any of the large number of military personnel present, perhaps angered at the players' tantrums which paled into insignificance in comparison to the type of life and death situations they had recently faced. In the end peace was eventually restored but the final result of 3-1 to Juventus seemed irrelevant after the day's events which were a shameful way in which to pay respect to Marchi.

The supersquad of Italy 1945-46

With the ending of the war, the Fascists fell from power and the former dictator Mussolini was publicly hanged in Milan. Most Italians had hoped that the decline of the fascist regime would bring more freedom and allow them to express themselves once more in thought, word and deed without fear of the recriminations to which they had grown accustomed. The new Democratics were busy creating a fresh political climate and any Italian of right-wing sympathy was considered a revolutionary. In this changing political environment Italy was starting anew and in still turbulent times and among many mixed emotions football appeared to Italians as a symbol of hope and a sign of normality. It was a practical demonstration that life could carry on and that it was possible to flourish again despite the awful times that people had lived through. As football entered the psyche once more, many teams reverted to their original names, such as Ambrosiana who returned to the more familiar Inter. Newspapers were back in circulation again, this time without the censorship afforded by the Fascist regime and the new paper *Tutto Sport*, published in Turin, took off thanks to its founder, the journalist Renato Casalbore.

After leaving their home ground in the war years to play at the Velodromo, Torino were back at the Filadelfia with Ferruccio Novo quick to strengthen the team once more. During the war championship, Novo had realised that his side was in need of an overhaul and with this in mind he decided to improve its defensive capabilities. Thus, in the summer of 1945 new players were brought to the club. Torino were already blessed with an abundance of attacking players but lacked a defensive solidity which would allow the forward players to flourish even more. Novo's purchases were to create a near-perfect formation. In came goalkeeper Bacigalupo from Savona, the Triestina full-back Aldo Ballarin, the midfielder Mario Rigamonti from Brescia and the young Virgilio Maroso from Alessandria. The final purchase for the inaugural post-war championship was the Spezia midfielder Eusebio Castigliano. Meanwhile, Romeo Menti was loaned to Fiorentina for one season, his place on the right wing being taken by Franco Ossola. Together with the already established Grezar, Loik, Mazzola, Gabetto and Ferraris – and with Zecca, Guaraldo, Santagiuliana and Piacentini in reserve – Torino had assembled a great squad of players, the Grande Torino.

With the war only recently ended, communications between regions had not yet been properly re-established and it was decided that the 1945-46 tournament be divided into two geographical groups, the Alta Italia and Centre South of Italy. The Final of the championship was to be contested between the first four teams of each group. Torino dominated the Northern section, winning the group with 42 points followed by Inter (39), Juventus (35) Milan (30) and were joined at the final stage by Napoli, winners of the Centre South group, along with Bari, Roma and Pro-Livorno.

During the first round of the tournament Torino had re-written the record books including the highest number of goals (65), of which 37 were scored by the trio of Loik, Gabetto and Mazzola. From the 26 matches played, 19 ended in victory including memorable wins over Genoa 6-0, Triestina 4-0 and Bologna 4-0. The opening fixture of the final round on 28 April 1946 matched Torino against their old adversaries Roma and this game signalled to the nation the phenomenon that Torino had become. A scintillating 7-0 win at the home of their rivals marked the realisation that a truly great team had emerged, a fact sportingly acknowledged in defeat by the Roma fans.

From that point Torino progressed strongly, including big wins over Napoli 7-1 and Inter 6-2, but needed to be wary of an emerging threat from Juventus. In the first leg of the derby Juventus won a tight match 1-0, thanks to a goal from the former Torino player Silvio Piola who had joined them that season. The second leg saw a reversal of the scoreline with a solitary strike from Gabetto ensuring a vital victory and revenge for the earlier defeat. It was also the penultimate match and the result left Torino and Juventus locked together on 20 points. On 28 July 1946, Torino hammered Livorno 9-1 at the Filadelfia while Juventus could only manage a draw against Napoli. Novo's planning had paid off and once again the Scudetto was in his hands. Due to events surrounding the ending of the war, the tournament had started in October and concluded at the end of July. This meant that it was impossible for the Federation to organise the Coppa Italia for that season and Torino were thus denied the chance of another double triumph.

The third Scudetto of Il Grande Torino, 1946-47

With football once again firmly established and the country slowly returning to some semblance of order, the championship resumed as Serie A in 1946-47. During the close season Novo again introduced new faces to boost the squad including goalkeeper Dante Piani, full-back Francesco Rosetta, midfielder Danilo Martelli and centre-forward Guido Tieghi. The new arrivals bolstered an already formidable squad but the opening matches of the new campaign saw a poor return on the investment with a 1-1 home draw against Triestina and 1-0 defeat at Venezia. Adding to the early season problems was goalkeeper Bacigalupo who suffered a bad shoulder injury and was replaced by the new recruit, Piani. When Bacigalupo regained fitness, coach Luigi Ferrero decided against putting him straight back into the team, instead keeping faith with Piani. For Bacigalupo the move came as a shock but to his credit he took the decision well and set about forcing his way back into the team.

The turning point of the season came with the goalless draw against Juventus on 20 October 1946. Following the derby match, Torino reeled off 11 consecutive victories, the winning run continuing up to 19 January 1947 when it was halted by a 2-0 defeat at Alessandria. This defeat proved to be only a temporary blip, however, with wins quickly being registered against Milan 2-1, Triestina 1-0 and Lazio 5-1. The next match saw another defeat, 3-1 at the hands of Sampdoria, which proved the final loss of the season. From 9 March 1947 through to the end of the championship, Torino dropped only two further points, with draws against Bologna 1-1 and Bari 0-0 being interspersed with an amazing 14 victories. Some impressive scores included wins over Inter 5-2, Vicenza 6-0, Fiorentina 4-0, Genoa 6-0, Milan 6-2 and victory over Juventus in the derby, 1-0 at the Stadio Comunale.

The most spectacular result of this eventful season, though, proved to be against Bologna in November at the Filadelfia. Bologna were leading the classifica with Torino four points behind them in the table. The importance of the fixture was reflected by the intensity of the atmosphere inside the stadium which inspired the Torino team to a crushing 4-0 win over the early-season pace setters. Goals from Castigliano, Ossola,

Ferraris and Loik had sent a chilling message to the rest of the league that Torino were in no mood to surrender their title.

The final league placings saw Torino finish with 63 points, ten points ahead of the runners-up Juventus. The season had seen Torino break through the century goal barrier, finishing with 104 league goals, 29 of them coming from Valentino Mazzola, the first time that a Torino wing-half had ended up as top scorer. The Torino squad had, without question, become the one that all other teams had somehow to emulate. In an attempt to keep up, the bigger teams in the league were now concentrating their efforts on strengthening their squads. The influence held by the Torino club over football in Italy had grown to the point where they were regarded nationally as the example to imitate not only on the pitch but also on a management and organisational level.

The national team become Granata

The dominance which the Grande Torino held on the domestic game in Italy spilled over into the international arena on 11 May 1947 when the Granata players effectively took on the guise of the national team. For the match against Hungary, ten Torino players featured in the starting line-up – and for good measure the fixture was played in Turin. The unlucky player to miss out on this historic occasion was the goalkeeper, Bacigalupo, whose individualistic style was considered too erratic for international football by the Azzurri coach Pozzo, who chose Juventus goalkeeper Sentimenti IV instead. It was a world record for ten players from the same club team to appear together at national level, although for the Italian public the selection was considered a formality in light of the brilliance of the Torino team.

For that reason the nature of this record-breaking achievement was lost on the majority of supporters, although they would have seen the irony of the match being played at the Stadio Comunale, home of Juventus, Torino's deadly rivals. In front of 73,000 spectators, Italy took an early lead through Gabetto, only for the scores to be levelled after the interval when Hungary scored through Szusza. A few minutes later another Gabetto goal restored Italy's lead but Hungary refused to accept defeat and with 15 minutes remaining the Magyars equalised for the second time, from the penalty spot after Ballarin had handled. The home fans, who had expected nothing less than victory for their side, grew restless, showing their displeasure with a series of jeers and whistles. Such behaviour puzzled some observers, considering that the vast majority of the crowd were Torino fans and that the home players, bar one notable exception, were the ones they were so used to cheering. However, in the last minute the atmosphere changed dramatically to one of celebration when Mazzola centred for Loik to score and give Italy the match, 3-2.

A footnote to the match was that although ten Torino players had featured in the starting line-up, initially only nine were scheduled to play. Originally Vittorio Pozzo had selected Carlo Parola, the centre midfield player from Juventus, but the day prior to the match Parola had appeared for the Rest of Europe side against a Great Britain team at Hampden Park, Glasgow, in a match arranged to celebrate the return of the four British associations to FIFA. Pozzo had made arrangements for the Juventus player to return to Turin the following day, but despite a 6-1 win for the British team, the Juventus star was afforded generous hospitality by some Italian immigrants in Glasgow. The partying continued well into the early hours and with the excesses of the evening taking their inevitable toll, Parola was unable to make his expected return early enough to feature in the international. In his place, Pozzo called up the Torino midfielder Mario Rigamonti for his international debut.

The historic nature of the match against Hungary was not to be repeated, certainly not on the same scale. For the next international, against Austria in Vienna on 9 November 1947, Pozzo decided on a different tactical approach, calling on only three Torino players, Mazzola, Maroso and Ballarin. The result was a resounding 5-1 win for Austria and a month later Pozzo changed course once more by selecting eight Torino players for the match against Czechoslovakia in Bari, including, rather oddly, goalkeeper Bacigalupo who had not been considered good enough some months earlier. Pozzo's decision was justified with goals from Torino's Menti and Gabetto paving the way for a 3-1 win. With more than a helping hand from the Grande Torino, the Italian national team had once more returned to winning ways.

A cover taken from a popular magazine of the 1940s picturing the squad of the Grande Torino.

The Grande Torino, taking time out to relax before the start of training.

Mazzola leads out the Grande Torino.

Bolmida, the legendary bugle player at the Filadelfia.

The 'mythical' Filadelfia Stadium.

Volunteers clear the snow
away from the Filadelfia pitch
the winter of 1948.

Pietro Ferraris,
winner of four
Scudettos with the
Grande Torino.

The rebel, Mario Rigamonti pictured with his second passion, his motorbike.

A classic pose from goalkeeper Valerio Bacigalupo.

Mr Versatile, Danilo Martelli.

Guglielmo Gabetto (left) and Franco Ossola, partners on the pitch and in business.

The Grande Torino, as seen by the popular Italian cartoonist Signor Silva.

The Grande Torino are applauded as they take to the field at the Filadelfia.

The popular Trio Nizza (pictured from left) of Bacigalupo, Martelli and
Rigamonti were never far away from entertainment. Here, they are pictured at
a Turin radio studio where Martelli performed a song.

27 April 1947, Italy v Switzerland. Nine players of the
Grande Torino line up to play for the national team.

A Team In Demand

WITH an established squad of international players hungry to continue their amazing run of success, the omens looked good for the defence of the title in 1947-48. However, preparations were hit when one of the key players, Mario Rigamonti, failed to appear for the first pre-season training session. Such an event was not considered uncommon as Rigamonti would regularly take off on his motorbike and disappear for days, so the general consensus among the players was that he was taking an extended holiday in the Liguria Riviera. So, as the new season beckoned, preparations carried on without Rigamonti, with a full-scale practice match organised at the Filadelfia in order for Egri Erbstein to decide which players would figure in the first team squad.

The trial was important for the youth players who saw it as the ideal opportunity to impress the coach and force their way into the senior set-up. Among those waiting to grab their chance was the young Sauro Toma who, due to the absence of Rigamonti, took the position of stopper with Ballarin on his left and Maroso on his right. In front of them were Grezar and Castigliano, complementing the attacking power of Menti, Loik, Gabetto, Mazzola and Ferraris. For the first time in his career, Toma was appearing in front of the watchful eyes of some of the Torino faithful. Although the game was only a practice match, many fans took an early opportunity to catch a glimpse of the team in action, the passion of the supporters knowing no bounds. Despite playing alongside the stars of the Grande Torino, Toma was not overawed and performed well, receiving encouragement from his peers. It was clear to Toma from this first-hand introduction why the Torino side was so special. Their greatness appeared to come as much from the deep feeling of togetherness in the squad as it did from the talents of its many gifted individuals. This collective spirit, harnessed to the great individual skills which ran through the team, made the side one which everyone, including Toma, wanted to be part of.

With time running out before the first match of the season, and with Erbstein and

Copernico still unaware of Rigamonti's whereabouts, a new name needed to be penciled into the starting line-up. The circumstances should have presented the perfect opportunity for Toma to make his debut in Serie A, but unfortunately he was carrying over a suspension from the last match of the previous season. While playing for La Spezia in Serie B, Toma had traded blows with the Viareggio centre-forward, Vinicio Viani, and consequently received a ban. His suspension only added to the woes of the Torino coaching staff who were running out of time to find a replacement for Rigamonti. Their situation was not helped by the fact that Franco Ossola had been involved in a car accident and suffered injuries bad enough to prevent him from appearing in the opening matches.

For their opening fixture Torino had to face Napoli at the Filadelfia, but on the day of the match there was still no sign of Rigamonti. Copernico took the brave decision to select a youth team player, Biglino, but just an hour before kick-off, and to everyone's astonishment, Rigamonti appeared in the home dressing-room. Looking fit and relaxed he offered a few words of apology to Copernico and Erbstein before pulling on the familiar burgundy shirt and minutes later ran out on to the pitch to join the rest of his teammates. This amazing sequence of events had no unsettling effect on the team with Torino winning at a canter, 4-0 with goals from Menti, Gabetto, Mazzola and Ferraris.

Despite the winning start, Rigamonti himself had a very poor game, committing a series of fouls due to his lack of proper match fitness. Although breathing a huge sigh of relief at his return, Erbstein decided that Rigamonti needed a couple of weeks' hard training to restore his fitness. The following match, against Bari, presented a chance for the young Sauro Toma to make his long-awaited Serie A debut. On arrival at the Bari stadium, Toma's big day was shattered by the news that Rigamonti had been given a reprieve and selected in his place. Feeling upset, and in a state of disbelief, Toma asked for an explanation. Novo, an acknowledged expert in man management, told him that, being young, there would be plenty of future opportunities in the first team but that for the present Rigamonti remained an automatic choice.

Whether Novo's words eased Toma's pain at missing out on his debut, no one knows. What is certain is that neither Toma nor Torino would remember the day with any affection as a goal from the Bari wing-half Tavellin condemned them to a 1-0 defeat. Rigamonti was sent off in the second half, so at least for Toma the path was now clear for him to play in the next match.

Preparing for the following fixture against Lucchese, Erbstein took time to pin-point the tactics they would deploy in an attempt to get back on the winning trail. Lucchese were known as an adventurous team but technically average, so Erbstein's plan was to play a counter-attacking game. The strategy worked to perfection with Torino sweeping away their opponents 6-0 with goals from Loik (2), Mazzola, Gabetto,

Ballarin and Castigliano. The following week they repeated the performance with a staggering 7-1 win over Roma in the Olympic Stadium. And as the season progressed, a pattern was set with some big home wins, including victories over Salernitana 7-1, Inter 5-0 and Triestina 6-0, being offset by a sprinkling of away defeats including Bologna 1-0, Atalanta 1-0 and 3-2 at the San Siro against Milan.

The slight dip in consistency was not helped by the absence through injury of Maroso and Castigliano. Although Toma and fellow reserve player Fabian performed admirably, the absence of the two stars was instrumental in lifting the morale of the opposition. Maroso returned to the team on 1 February 1948 in the 3-0 win at Modena, a victory which heralded a prolific run of form. Wins included those over Bari 5-1, Roma 4-1, Vicenza 4-0 and Bologna 5-1 before the run culminated on 2 May 1948 with a record-breaking 10-0 victory against Alessandria at the Filadelfia. In between this tremendous surge, Torino had battled out a tough 1-1 draw against Juventus at the Comunale, the scoreline being a repeat of the encounter at the Filadelfia earlier in the season. Going into the last quarter of the campaign, Torino opened up an almost unassailable lead and needed only to hold their nerve to retain the title.

A week after the Alessandria massacre, Torino met Inter at the San Siro. The Inter side contained two great attacking players: Achilli, who was nicknamed *gamba di sedano* (celery leg) and Lorenzi, who was known as *veleno* (poison). Achilli possessed a great turn of pace which enabled him to accelerate past opposing defenders, while Lorenzi was regarded as a 'pirate' in the penalty area, throwing himself to the ground at every opportunity. His actions made Toma, who was assigned the task of marking him, very nervous, with Lorenzi falling to the ground everytime Toma made a tackle. At first the Roman referee, Gemini, appeared to ignore Lorenzi's histrionics, although he booked Toma, much to the pleasure of the Inter supporters. However, as the game wore on, the referee grew tired of Lorenzi's play-acting and apologised to Toma. In the end Mazzola ensured justice was done by scoring the only goal of the game to give Torino both points. On the same Sunday, Torino's nearest challengers, Milan, were defeated by Juventus at the Comunale.

The Torino team were now riding on the crest of a wave, their confidence sky-high, and the following week they crushed Atalanta 4-0. After a goalless draw at Triestina, the Granata embarked upon a magnificent run, maintaining a 100 per cent record to the end of the season, although that record was placed under severe threat during a tremendous encounter against Lazio at the Filadelfia on 30 May 1948. An inspired opening 20 minutes saw Lazio lead the champions elect 3-0 with goals from their attackers Penzo and Puccinelli along with a Grezar own-goal. The Filadelfia fans could not believe their eyes and urged on their team with a passion rarely before witnessed at the stadium. The players responded to this electric atmosphere with Castigliano pulling a goal back before half-time. In the second half, after a period of incessant pressure, they drew level through Castigliano again and Gabetto. Both team and crowd sensed that a remarkable victory was now possible and Mazzola provided the required spark of genius, scoring a brilliant solo goal to seal a remarkable comeback. This game, as much as all the high-scoring victories, proved once and for all the great ability of the Torino team to dig deep into their reserve and strength of character to overcome the most unlikely odds.

Another goal glut occurred the following week with a 5-2 triumph over Livorno, with another two points clinched seven days later at the Marassi Stadium against old adversaries, Genoa. The match, won 2-1 by Torino, was a real battle which proved to be one of the most difficult games of their season. During the first half, with Torino leading 1-0, the Genoa centre-forward, Brighenti, had upset goalkeeper Bacigalupo with some challenges which many referees might not have allowed. For a time Bacigalupo tolerated the physical threat posed by Brighenti, accepting his presence as part of the perils he faced as a goalkeeper, but in the second half, following a series of particularly heavy challenges, his patience snapped and he punched the Genoa player in the face. Referee Belle had no choice but to dismiss Bacigalupo and Torino found themselves not only down to ten men but without a recognised goalkeeper.

At this point Mazzola assumed control and, without uttering a word, picked up Bacigalupo's gloves and took up his position between the posts. Thereafter Mazzola performed as if the role was natural to him, his calm, assertive manner spreading through the team. The first save he was called upon to make saw him punch the ball with so much power that it almost reached the halfway line, no mean feat in those days of heavy footballs. Inspired by their captain, goals from Castigliano and Gabetto cancelled out a reply from the Genoa midfielder Bergamo but the real man of the match was Mazzola. The ill feeling which the teams displayed on the pitch erupted later off the field when some Genoa fans waited for the Torino players outside the dressing-rooms. The Torino stars were forced to run a gauntlet of abuse and used their luggage bags as protection against the various objects hurled by irate Genoa fans. Eventually, police dispersed the crowd but not before the windows of the Torino 'Conte Rosso' bus had been smashed, thus ensuring a cold and draughty journey back to Turin, although the warm glow of victory probably made the journey more tolerable.

Champions again

After this match Torino were crowned champions of Italy again although they still had two games left to play at the Filadelfia, against Milan and Modena. Crowds flocked to the stadium, keen that the celebrations would last for what remained of the season. Milan, the eventual runners-up, were locked in a battle for second place with Juventus and Triestina and were in no mood to be part of the carnival atmosphere. After a tight encounter, Torino eventually emerged victorious 2-1, with goals from Gabetto and Ossola. For the last match of the season, against Modena on 27 June 1948, the fans created a wonderful atmosphere at the Filadelfia with Bolmida, the local stationmaster, playing his bugle in unison with the noise of the crowd.

The fans had gorged on success at the Filadelfia and, amazingly, had not seen Torino defeated there in a league match for five years, the last team to come away from the stadium with both points being Ambrosiana (Inter) on 17 January 1943. Since that defeat Torino had played a total of 64 matches with 56 wins and eight draws, a remarkable statistic by any standard. The figure was improved upon still further with another big win, 5-2 over Modena, rounding off the season in emphatic style. Goals from Martelli (2), Loik, Castigliano and Menti ensured the celebrations were carried over well into the next few days, a suitable way to record a fourth consecutive Scudetto.

During the 1947-48 season, Torino had achieved some unique records, their final points tally of 65 being a record for Serie A as was the 16-point advantage they held over runners-up Milan. Added to a total of 125 goals scored and the 10-0 victory over Alessandria, it had truly been a record-breaking season. With a squad of players relatively tender in years, and with the club still hungry for success, nothing appeared to bar the way to further glories.

Torino conquest Brazil

With a fourth Scudetto won in such emphatic fashion, Ferruccio Novo received invitations from clubs around the world keen to play friendly matches against his Grande Torino team. After careful consideration, Novo accepted an attractive offer to tour Brazil, believing a trip to South America would be more prestigious for the club, given that football there was regarded with a fervour unmatched elsewhere. The tour itinerary consisted of four matches, including two evening kick-offs. The clubs providing the opposition were Sao Paulo, Corinthians, Portuguesa and Palmeiras, with the matches taking place between 18-28 July.

For the tour, the Alessandria player Cecco Rosetta was invited to join the party and the entire squad, with the exception of the masseur Ottavio Cortina who was scared of flying, made the trip. From Turin the party headed to Rome where they took a Panair flight which, after stopping at Dakar and Recife, landed at Rio de Janeiro in the early afternoon. Arriving at Rio, the party had to change aircraft, and boarded a Dakota to the city of Sao Paulo, much to the distaste of Rigamonti who had felt sick during the previous flight and needed assistance from the crew's doctor. The Dakota was an older model and appeared to be in poor condition, so much so that the idea of travelling in it scared still further those players less confident of flying. Most of the group suffered sickness during the trip, particularly when the plane encountered severe turbulence when passing over a mountain range. When the Dakota eventually landed at the airport of Cougonha it was to the great relief of everyone on board and their spirits were raised further by the sight of the 8,000 fans waiting to greet them.

The first match of the tour was against Palmeiras, who, to Torino's surprise, knew a great deal about them, thanks to the presence in their side of the former Inter midfielder Bovio. The game ended in a 1-1 draw with Gabetto scoring for Torino, but it was Toma who drew most praise with his performance meriting several pages of interviews in the local press. The second fixture against Corinthians was an evening kick-off. The Corinthians team was very strong and posed many problems on the night, in particular the centre-forward Baltazar who gave the Torino defence a torrid time. This time another goal from Gabetto was not enough to prevent a 2-1 defeat and from this point Torino realised they were facing some very talented opposition and that it was time to remind the hosts of their skills.

For the opening two matches of the tour, the players had been suffering the after-effects of their dreadful journey and tiredness caused by the different time zone. Now they were better acclimatised, coach Sperone devised a split training schedule, working the team in the morning with a second session in the early evening. Torino immediately benefited from the new routine, beating Portuguesa 4-1 with goals from Mazzola, Ossola, Castigliano and Gabetto.

Fireworks against Sao Paulo

The finale of the tour, against Sao Paulo, proved the greatest challenge, particularly as living in that city were many Italians for whom the game was desperately important. Additionally the Brazilian team included in their line-up the legendary Leonidas, the 'black pearl', a star of the 1938 World Cup. Heavy rain, which hammered down on the stadium as the 10pm kick-off approached, failed to dampen the wild enthusiasm of the spectators who welcomed the teams on to the pitch with a crescendo of noise. Above the stadium was the spectacle of the night sky lit up by a barrage of exploding fireworks, adding to an already intimidating atmosphere.

The celebrations led to the kick-off being delayed for 30 minutes, and when the match eventually got under way it was clear that the Sao Paulo team had no intention of treating the game as a friendly. It soon developed into a very physical affair with the Brazilians matching their subtle skills with a hard, uncompromising approached to stop their Italian counterparts. One Brazilian player in particular, called Ponce de Leon, took the fight to Torino almost single-handedly, upsetting Bacigalupo with a late challenge. Despite the provocation, Torino managed to take the lead and although enjoying the majority of the possession, Sao Paulo were unable to conjure up an equalising goal.

As the game wore on, Bacigalupo elected to take retribution on Ponce de Leon and waited his moment before throwing a punch straight on the Brazilian's chin. Chaos followed with Brazilian fans, angered at Bacigalupo's action, threatening to invade the pitch. Fearing for their safety, the Torino team ran to their dressing-room, hoping that the crowd would calm down. In the tunnel there was incredible confusion with everyone seemingly wanting to attack the Torino players and in particular Bacigalupo. Fortunately for the Italians, armed policemen were deployed to guard them until the situation improved. However, when the players re-emerged from the sanctuary of their dressing-room, no official appeared willing to take responsibility for protecting the visiting players.

The situation was chaotic. It seemed it would be impossible to continue the game because by now the crowd had invaded the pitch, yet any thoughts of postponing the match would only incense the crowd more and cause the likelihood of further trouble. After some heated debate, the decision was taken to resume the match, not least because the heavy rain teeming down on to the pitch had driven the spectators back to the shelter of the stands. Eventually, in an attempt to calm matters, an announcement was made that the match would restart with the expulsion of Bacigalupo and a penalty against Torino. The Granata coach, Sperone, had meanwhile replaced his disgraced goalkeeper with the substitute Bani, whose first task was to face the penalty taken by Ponce de Leon. To his credit, Bani anticipated the kick and saved the penalty with his head, although the impact of the shot resulted in a head injury that required treatment. In the end the match finished 2-2 with the referee disallowing a perfectly valid goal from Gabetto, a decision which no doubt was designed to stop the home fans from rioting.

A rocky journey home

Apart from the brawl against Sao Paulo, the Brazilian tour was heralded a great success and Novo rewarded each player with the sum of 100,000 lire and a pair of new shoes. For the journey back to Turin the players relived the nightmare of the previous flight with the homeward trip proving even more hazardous. From Sao Paulo, the party took the same Dakota plane, changing at Rio where they embarked on an Argentinian aircraft. Shortly after taking off the pilot discovered that the weight of the plane's cargo was in excess of its safety capacity and flying over Rio de Janeiro realised he could not accelerate properly. He decided to land immediately, forcing the Torino party to spend the ensuing night in a hotel.

Many of the squad were unable to sleep after the frightening experience they had endured earlier in the day, but the following morning assurances were given by the authorities that the plane assigned to take them home had undertaken the most stringent security checks. Once more the party boarded the aircraft, which stopped at Casablanca and Paris before finally landing in Turin. Only a day before the Torino party had left Sao Paulo, a plane had crashed into the Atlantic Ocean killing 75 passengers. On hearing the news upon their arrival in Turin, the players decided that they had enough of flying for the time being.

The last Scudetto of the Grande Torino, 1948-49

As a new season dawned, everyone connected with the club looked forward to emulating the successes of the previous seasons. After four consecutive championships, each one harbouring its own special memories, the Scudetto was to remain with the Granata once more although this time with terrible consequences.

Following the record-breaking achievements of 1947-48, there was a feeling among certain factions within the club that while the team had hit new heights, there was also the danger that a peak had been reached and that it would be difficult to maintain. The success of the last few seasons had been based on an evolving squad system, carefully manufactured to ensure the continuity of the team whenever a player was reaching the end of his career. The vanguard of the Grande Torino – Mazzola, Loik, Menti and Grezar – were now reaching their 30s, while Gabetto would be 32 in February.

With this in mind, Novo turned his attention to younger players who could learn from the great champions like Mazzola until the right opportunity arose for them to be integrated into the team. Novo also decided to open the door to the international market by bringing into the squad the Italian-French player Emile Bongiorni and the Hungarian-born Julius Schubert. In addition to the new imports came more home-based talent including midfielder Rubens Fadini, goalkeeper Dino Ballarin (the brother of Aldo), winger Ruggero Grava and the Turin-born defender Pierino Operto. Emphasis was also placed on the youth set-up and to assist with the development of the youth players Novo appointed as coach Oberdan Ussello from the Biella club, along with the Englishman Leslie Lievesely. Apart from the departure of 36-year-old Piero Ferraris to Novara, the rest of the squad remained unchanged from the previous season and with the new additions confidence in the camp was sky high for another successful season.

Preparations for the new season were conducted at the Filadelfia with Novo quickly being able to reach agreement with the players over salaries and winning bonuses. As shrewd as ever, Novo anticipated the players' requests and set about improving the rewards for the entire squad. Novo worked on the theory that a happy, well-paid squad was a winning one, and contracts were drawn up permitting each player to receive 1,500,000 lire for being part of the first team with an additional monthly salary of 100,000 lire, and 750,000 lire as a final winning bonus. As captain, Valentino Mazzola received special privileges and was awarded a bigger salary and extra bonuses. Such was his stature that the other players were happy to go along with the arrangement.

An ambitious plan thwarted in its infancy

To accommodate the players' wage rises and to ensure a sound base for future successes, Novo, together with Erbstein, developed an ambitious idea to improve the financial situation of the Torino club. Their vision was to build two different sides, one to play in the domestic championship and the other to play in the ever-growing lucrative market of international friendly matches like the ones they had contested in Brazil just a few months previously.

However, their plans were not helped by the new political problems which were enveloping Italy. The chaos surrounding the elections of 18 April 1948 was so far-reaching that the Communists and Socialists decided to unify, creating a People's Front party (*Fronte Popolare*) to defeat the Christian Democrats (*Democrazia Cristiana*). Any victory for the left wing would compromise the Marshall Plan, the scheme by which the United States gave economic aid to European countries trying to rebuild their economies in the aftermath of a war which had ravaged the continent. It was understood that the Americans would intervene militarily if there was a breakdown of law and order.

The tension finally exploded on 14 July when the MP Palmiro Togliatti, leader of the PCI (*Partito Comunista Italiano*) was shot by a Sicilian student outside the Montecitorio Palace in Rome. Immediately, civil war broke out with the Communist headquarters damaged and a general strike proclaimed. Working men occupied all the factories in the north of Italy, including the Fiat factory in Turin where some of the directors were kept hostage. Bizarrely, amid the political unrest came the announcement that the Italian cyclist Gino Bartali had won the Tour de France, and Communists and Democrats found themselves united in applauding Bartali in his achievement. Sport once again both united and divided the people. Bartali and Juventus were seen as the symbol of the Democrats while the other popular cyclist of the era, Fausto Coppi, and Torino were linked with the left wing. With the political upheaval, Novo was forced to abandon his idea and concentrate instead on capturing another Scudetto.

Business as usual but a bad injury

The 1948-49 season began well for Torino who beat Pro Patria 4-1 at the Filadelfia. Maroso was injured during the match and replaced by Sauro Toma who suffered a blow to his left knee later in the game. After a long wait for his chance in the first team, Toma asked to play in the following match against Atalanta even though he knew he was not fully fit. Torino lost that match 3-2 and shortly afterwards, during a training session, Toma decided to speak to the coach, the Englishman Leslie Lievesley, about his injury problem. In an attempt to diagnose the extent of the injury, Lievesley ordered Toma to undertake a series of kicking exercises. In attempting to retrieve one of the balls which had ended up in the stand at the Filadelfia, Toma fell over with the full weight of his body exerting pressure on his already painful knee. Feeling a sharp pain, Toma yelled out loud, convincing Lievesley that he had a serious problem. The knee soon became badly swollen and Toma was taken home by taxi and the following day was seen by Dr Micheli, the official doctor of the Torino club. After consulting with different specialists, the doctor decided to drain some fluid from Toma's knee but although the pain eased, Toma was still in no position to play football for a while. The doctor suggested various remedies including massage, injections and even the use of soda, but despite his advice the knee showed no signs of improvement. Toma's morale was low; he sensed that it would be a long time before he could play again.

With Toma injured, the door opened for Pierino Operto to make his debut in the next match, against Roma which Torino won 4-0. Operto played well enough to retain his place and a week later featured in the 2-0 win at Livorno. It was now a full eight months since Maroso had last played but despite his absence, the defensive strength in depth in the squad had ensured that the equilibrium had been maintained. During the season Torino suffered several other injury problems, most notably to Castigliano, Menti and Operto, but still managed to keep winning. After beating Lucchese 2-1, came the satisfaction of the same scoreline over Juventus at the Comunale with the derby success followed by a convincing 3-1 win over Padova. Six wins out of seven had suggested that Torino were going to run away with the championship again but a 1-0 defeat at the San Siro on 4 November 1948, against Milan, gave hope to the chasing pack.

The Milan match was a highly competitive game with Ballarin sent off, meaning that through injury and suspension the Torino club was quickly running out of full-backs. In desperation, Erbstein and Lievesley decided to call Maroso back into the fray, telephoning him at his apartment in the early hours. They told him of the crisis they faced and after a long discussion it was agreed that Maroso would travel to Florence to see a specialist, Dr Scaglietti, to seek approval to play again. The following morning, Maroso set off for Florence and 24 hours later turned up at the Filadelfia with a letter from the doctor authorising a return to action. Erbstein's decision was justified in the next fixture on 7 November 1948 when, with Martelli, Maroso and Fadini playing well together, Torino beat Lazio 1-0 at the Filadelfia, thanks to a goal from Mazzola.

An unstoppable machine

As the season passed into the winter months, two teams, Lucchese and Inter, emerged as the main rivals to Torino's bid for another title. The former virtually eliminated themselves from the race by losing at Genoa and Milan, while Inter kept within touching distance despite a 4-2 defeat at the Filadelfia on 12 December. With a two-point advantage over their main rivals, Torino were firmly on track for their fifth Scudetto but suffered a bleak Christmas when losing 3-0 at Genoa on 26 December 1948. Missing from the Torino line-up were the familiar names of Rigamonti, Castigliano, Loik, Ossola and Toma, and Erbstein had to call up Pietro Biglino, Pierino Operto and Luigi Giuliano as replacements. The changes disrupted the balance of the side with Genoa exploiting the situation to the full, putting on a fine performance in front of the home fans at the Marassi Stadium. The disappointment of the defeat was soon forgotten three days later, however, when goals from Menti and the returning Ossola ensured a 2-0 win over Bari. Torino ended their monumental year of 1948 on a happy note with everything in place for a repeat performance in the new year of 1949.

A 2-2 draw at Palermo on 6 January started a 16-match unbeaten run which lead into the decisive and penultimate encounter of the Grande Torino against Inter on 30 April 1949. The run included ten wins and six draws and although the victories were not as freescoring as in the previous season, a greater consistency was achieved with many wins by the odd goal. The most notable victory came in the derby on 13 February when Juventus were dispatched 3-1 at the Filadelfia through goals by Loik (2) and Gabetto. Although Torino had held the upper hand over the last few seasons, many of the derby matches had ended in draws, the intensity of the occasion often producing stalemate between the sides. Coming on the back of the 2-1 win achieved at the Comunale back in October, the derby success was particularly pleasing, especially for the fans who were anxious to see their club remain number one in Turin and Italy. As the team and supporters celebrated this latest success no one knew how poignant the victory was to be.

After the rigours of the derby, Torino played out an incredible 4-4 draw at Padova, coming from behind to earn a valuable point thanks to goals from Menti (2), Ossola and Castigliano. Big wins soon followed against Milan 4-1 and Novara 4-0 with further draws achieved at Lazio 2-2 and Triestina 1-1, leaving Torino on course for another title.

On 17 April 1949, once more Torino took to the field at the Filadelfia, a ground where they had enjoyed a phenomenal run of success dating back to 1942. On their home pitch, Torino had proved invincible and again turned on the style, treating the fans to yet another victory, 3-1 against Modena, with goals from Mazzola, Menti and Ballarin. As the players made their way down the tunnel after taking the applause of the crowd, no one present could possibly have imagined this would be the last glimpse of their heroes on the sacred soil of the Filadelfia. The following week a goal from Mazzola earned another valuable point at Bari to set up a decisive match against second-placed Inter at the San Siro, a fixture clouded in controversy due to a commitment overseas.

The Grande Torino pictured w[ith] the famous Italian cyclist Faus[to] Coppi (pictured second from right) after enjoying a meal at Il Cervo restaurant in Turin.

The fame of the Grande Torino led [to] them being the subject of various magazine articles not connected w[ith] football. Here, Ezio Loik together w[ith] (from left) Ballarin, Ossola and Ga[bli] are reading such an article dedicat[ed to] them in the popular magazine *Il T[empo]*.

Ezio Loik (left) and Valerio Bacigalupo enjoying a momen[t] of relaxation.

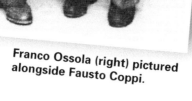

Franco Ossola (right) pictured alongside Fausto Coppi.

The Grande Torino, pictured in Rome with the famous Italian actress of the 1940s, Doris Durante.

e Torino club received many offers to play friendly matches abroad. Here the squad is tured boarding the Panair plane for the trip to Brazil in July 1948.

The
arrival of
the
Grande
Torino in
Sao Paulo,
Brazil 1948.

The
Grande
Torino at
the
banquet
organised
in their
honour
welcoming
them to
Brazil.

Ezio Loik (left), known as 'the engine', one of the fittest players in the squad seen preparing for pre-season training at the Filadelfia.

Valentino Mazzola (left) pictured with his great Juventus adversary Carlo Parola.

Superga Farewell

TORINO had dominated the domestic game in Italy throughout the 1940s. Their innovation and brilliance, coupled with the sheer talent of their individual players, had also been recognised at international level. With the regular winning of the Scudetto, the Grande Torino players had forged the backbone of the national team, the Azzurri. International football was an opportunity to enhance reputations and create contacts with other great European teams and in May 1949 Torino embarked on a prestigious friendly in Lisbon against Benfica, a football match of monumental outcome.

The idea for the match was born at an international fixture played on 27 February 1949 between Italy and Portugal in Genoa, which the Azzurri won 4-1. The captain of the Portugal team, Francisco Ferreira, who was regarded as one of the greatest players of the era, was shortly due to retire from the game. At the end of the match, Ferreira approached Valentino Mazzola, his Italian counterpart and a player he greatly respected. As a great admirer of the Grande Torino, the Portuguese player asked Mazzola if he would bring his Torino team to Lisbon to play a friendly match against his club side, Benfica, to mark his farewell to football. Mazzola, an honourable man as well as a great footballer, agreed to the request, recognising that the salaries being earned in Italy were way beyond the imagination of the Portuguese players. By many standards Portugal was a poor country and a football match between Benfica and the mighty Torino would create much interest and generate a sufficient amount of money for Ferreira's retirement. At the time not many club sides enjoyed the luxury of playing abroad, although Torino never refused the opportunity to travel around the world for games, having of course undertaken the trip to Brazil the previous year.

For the match to become a reality, Mazzola first had to seek approval from Ferruccio Novo. The president, however, did not warm to the idea, pointing out to Mazzola that the championship took priority over any friendly match. A month later, on 27 March 1949, Ferreira and Mazzola met again in Madrid at the international between Spain and Italy, won 3-1 by the Italians. The two players discussed the merits of the match with Novo, who by now had come to a compromise and agreed to let the squad go to Lisbon providing that they did not lose the forthcoming key league fixture against Inter at the San Siro. The trio established details for the match including the date, which was set for Tuesday, 3 May 1949.

In order for the game in Portugal to go ahead, the match against Inter needed to be brought forward a day from Sunday to Saturday. Initially, this created some problems but Mazzola, having given his word to Ferreira, had no intention of letting the Portuguese star down. The idea of a trip to Lisbon had also captured the imagination of the entire Torino squad, who shared Mazzola's enthusiasm for the match. Following some delicate negotiations, the club managed to obtain permission from the Italian League to change the date of the Inter fixture. The decision was reluctantly accepted by Inter who, being in second position behind Torino, saw the game as their last chance to reduce the deficit and keep alive their slim hopes of winning the Scudetto. The match controversially went ahead on Saturday, 30 April with a crowd of 36,000 watching the teams contest a hard-fought goalless draw. Ironically Mazzola was unable to take part in the game due to a late bout of 'flu. Also missing through injury was Virgilio Maroso, so overall a draw was considered a good result for Torino. With only four league matches remaining, the squad headed to Lisbon confident of another championship success and looking forward to a well-earned break in the Portuguese sunshine.

After contacting their families later that night, the squad settled in preparation for the flight to Lisbon which was to leave from Milan the following morning. As the departure time of midday approached, some confusion occurred around a group of journalists keen on following the team on the trip. As there were a limited number of seats on the plane several of them had to be turned away, leaving some angry and disappointed reporters, including Nino Oppio from the *Corriere di Milano*, who begged his friend, Mazzola, to find him a seat. Also unable to make the trip was Sauro Toma, whose knee injury had ruled him out for the rest of the season. The other casualty, Virgilio Maroso, was still some way short of match fitness but remained determined to go and took his place on board. At the last minute the reserve goalkeeper, Renato Gandolfi, was persuaded to stand down in favour of Dino Ballarin, on the pretence that the trip would provide valuable experience for the young protégé. Unknown to Gandolfi, Ballarin's elder brother, Aldo, had used his status as a senior member of the squad to influence the Torino management to allow his brother to join him. Away from the playing staff a notable absentee was Ferruccio Novo who was recovering from a minor operation. He had reluctantly approved the trip after initially rejecting the idea, a decision which was to haunt him in later years.

A cancelled trip for Bologna

A lesser known fact concerning that fateful Lisbon trip is that Bologna, not Torino, had initially been asked to play in honour of Ferreira. Benfica had close ties with the Bologna club which made them an obvious choice of opposition. In those days Bologna were a proud and successful team, having won four Scudettos between 1936 and 1941, a feat which had made the club popular abroad. An agreement had been reached by the two clubs with only the date and travel expenditure to be decided. However, when Portugal played Italy some weeks later, history was to change course when Ferreira met Mazzola. During the after-match banquet, organised to welcome the Portuguese team in Italy, the two captains had a long conversation. Mazzola learned of Ferreira's forthcoming testimonial and when the Portuguese player asked whether Torino might be interested in going to Lisbon, Mazzola agreed to do all he could to arrange it. The two men soon became friends and upon his return home, Ferreira informed the Benfica directors of his conversation with Mazzola. Although conscious that they had provisionally invited Bologna, the directors were enthusiastic about the prospect of the great Torino side coming to Lisbon and set about granting Ferreira's wish.

The change of opposition was confirmed when Italy played Spain in Madrid. Ferreira made the short plane trip to Madrid and at the training camp of the Azzurri at the Hotel Palace agreed the details with Mazzola and Novo. As a consequence of their actions, Bologna were informed of the change of plan. The president of Bologna, Renato Dall'Ara, had already booked a hotel for his squad and was himself intending to travel to Lisbon by car, using the match as an excuse to spend a holiday in Portugal. When informed of the decision that Torino had been invited instead, Dall'Ara exploded with anger, although his bitter disappointment would be overtaken by emotions of an altogether different kind on 4 May.

The feast that turned into tragedy

Due to severe turbulence the flight to Portugal was an unpleasant one and after stopping off at Barcelona to refuel, the aircraft landed at the Lisbon airport of Portela di Sacavem at 4.30pm. Upon arrival, the Torino party was met by a group of reporters and sporting celebrities, led by the Benfica captain Ferreira. On the way to their hotel the players took the opportunity to visit the beautiful Stadio Naçional where the match would be played. Built specifically to host the matches of the Portuguese national team, the grandeur of the stadium immediately impressed the Torino party who were already looking forward to showing off their skills to the Lisbon public.

On Monday, 2 May a light training session was arranged at 9.30am at the Estoril Plage, the home of Benfica, under the supervision of Leslie Lievesley. In the afternoon, at around 4.30pm, the players attended an official reception at the headquarters of the Benfica club where they were welcomed in a manner afforded to only great teams and players. Later that same afternoon, as a break from the rigours of their hectic schedule, the players were granted some free time to visit the city of Lisbon. Taking the opportunity to see the sights and to buy presents, some of them sent postcards to their families and loved ones, telling of the great time they were having. Unbeknown to them at the time was the tragic consequence their greetings would have when the cards arrived in Turin a few days later. After their short period of recreation the players attended a gala in the evening, hosted by Lisbon's mayor at the council buildings to officially welcome them to the city. The function, though, was relatively brief, allowing the team to return to their hotel reasonably early and prepare for the match the following day. As they lay their heads on their pillows that night, none of them could have known that this game would be their final curtain.

A last bow for the Grande Torino

On the morning of the match, 3 May 1949, hundreds of local people gathered outside the Hotel du Parque, where the players were guests, to greet the Grande Torino squad and wish them the best of luck for the match. On the way to the stadium Mazzola, Menti and Aldo Ballarin complained of feeling unwell but due to the contractual agreement made between the clubs there was no choice for them but to play. Torino had promised Benfica to field their full-strength team in order to attract as many fans as possible. However, despite the advance publicity, ticket sales had been slow, alarming the Benfica management who were relying on a big crowd to mark the special occasion. Any worries soon disappeared, though, when, shortly before kick-off, a huge crowd began to gather with almost 40,000 spectators filling the stadium to its capacity. To add to Ferreira's joy, two of the Torino directors, Rinaldo Agnisetta and Ippolito Civalleri, gave their Benfica colleagues a sum of money as a gift to the player on behalf of the Torino club. The Portuguese officials were not expecting such generosity and were moved by the gesture.

So, after much negotiation and effort on the part of both clubs, the game was at last ready to go ahead. The teams emerged on to the pitch to be met by a fantastic reception from the Benfica fans, the loudest cheers being reserved for Ferreira and Mazzola. Players on both sides joined in the applause for Ferreira before the captains exchanged handshakes and gifts to herald the start of the match. At 6pm the all-conquering Grande Torino team kicked-off one more time with this line-up: Bacigalupo, Ballarin, Martelli, Grezar, Rigamonti, Castigliano, Menti, Loik, Gabetto, Mazzola and Ossola.

The game itself was highly entertaining although lacking the fierce competitive edge associated with league or cup encounters. After Mazzola missed an open goal in the fourth minute, Torino opened the scoring when some fine interplay by Grezar, Menti and Gabetto allowed Ossola to make up for his captain's early error. Benfica quickly replied, equalising in the 23rd minute with a goal from Melao following a corner taken by Arsenio. The Portuguese team pressed on and eventually they took the lead through a headed goal from Arsenio in the 33rd minute. Their celebrations were cut short minutes later, however, when Torino levelled through substitute Bongiorni who had replaced the tired Gabetto. To cap a frantic spell of action, Melao added a third goal to make the half-time score 3-2 in Benfica's favour. The second half saw several scoring opportunities for both sides and with the minutes ticking away, Benfica added a fourth goal through Rogerio. In the dying seconds, Mazzola was upended in the penalty area, with the resultant spot-kick successfully converted by Menti to make the final score 4-3 to Benfica.

In the end the result was unimportant. The crowd had witnessed a highly entertaining spectacle and Ferreira had enjoyed the type of occasion for which he had been dreaming. The reputation of the Grande Torino as one of the great names in world football had also been suitably cemented in the hearts of the Lisbon public.

In the evening a dinner party was held in honour of Ferreira who received numerous gifts from a large gathering of well wishers. Before the party ended, Ferreira made a speech thanking the Torino club for their kindness and, as a mark of his gratitude, presented them with two large boxes of tuna fish and one box of sardines! With the function over, the Torino party retired to their hotel for some well-earned sleep, knowing they had to be early risers the next morning for the flight home.

The fatal flight

Although the trip had been relatively short, the hectic schedule had made it appear longer and as they departed from Lisbon, the Torino party looked forward to seeing family and friends again. On the Fiat G212 aircraft for the return flight to Turin were 31 passengers, consisting of 18 Torino players, two club directors, one technical coach, one trainer, one masseur, three journalists, one tour organiser and four members of the plane crew. The 18 players were (in alphabetical order): Valerio Bacigalupo, Aldo Ballarin, Dino Ballarin, Emile Bongiorni, Eusebio Castigliano, Rubens Fadini, Guglielmo Gabetto, Ruggero Grava, Giuseppe Grezar, Ezio Loik, Virgilio Maroso, Danilo Martelli, Valentino Mazzola, Romeo Menti, Piero Operto, Franco Ossola, Mario Rigamonti, Giulio Schubert.

The non-playing officials were the club directors Rinaldo Agnisetta and Ippolito Civalleri, the technical coach Ernest Egri Erbstein, the trainer Leslie Lievesley and the masseur Ottavio Cortina. The journalists were Renato Casalbore from *Tutto Sport*, Luigi Cavallero from *La Stampa*, and Renato Tosatti from *La Gazzetta del Popolo*. The other passengers on the flight were the tour organiser Andrea Bonaiuti and the crew consisting of the captain and first pilot Pierluigi Meroni, the second pilot Cesare Biancardi, and the flight engineers Antonio Pangrazi and Celestino D'Inca. They were all expected back in Turin at the Aeritalia airfield later that afternoon, 4 May 1949.

Although it was springtime, a heavy mist and torrential rain were covering the city of Turin where the local authorities had issued a bad weather warning. As they awaited the return of the Torino party, workers at the Aeritalia airfield were becoming increasingly concerned about the weather conditions. At 5.02pm, the pilot, Pierluigi Meroni, radioed a message to the Aeritalia field confirming that all was well and that they were approaching the outskirts of Turin, soon to begin their descent. The airfield immediately relayed a warning to the flight crew of the awful weather conditions in Turin, which Meroni acknowledged, replying that everything was under control. Three minutes later, at 5.05pm, staff at the airport, worried that they had heard nothing more, called the captain again but this time there was no answer. At this point the radio controller raised the alarm and contacted airports at Milan, Genoa, Alghero and Barcelona, asking if they had received any transmission from Meroni. The ensuing replies were negative. The G212 had disappeared from the sky.

At the same moment as the last radio message was sent, a builder living close to the hill of Superga situated outside Turin saw an aircraft emerge from the clouds and plummet straight into an embankment behind a nearby church. The monks attached to the church were accustomed to hearing the noise of aircraft flying over the building but this time, from inside the chapel, they felt the walls vibrate and saw what was later described as an 'intense sparkling light'. At first, they thought that a plane had hit the dome of their church and they rushed outside. One of the monks, Don Ricca, saw fragments of an aircraft and realised that something terrible had happened. It was obvious that the plane had been destroyed, leaving little or no chance of finding anyone alive. The scene that greeted the first rescuers was one of total carnage with mutilated and burnt bodies strewn among the wreckage across the field. Neither Don Ricca nor the other monks had any idea that the aircraft was carrying the Torino team. Only by opening a suitcase that was still intact and which must have fallen from the plane before it crashed, did one of the rescuers notice a burgundy shirt with the tricolour shield, the Scudetto of the Grande Torino.

The coffee never drunk

Vittore Catella, president of Juventus in the 1960s and today a man in his early 90s, was a former pilot who made test flights for the military during World War Two. Catella was a good friend of Pierluigi Meroni and together they had tested the Fiat G212 plane only a week previously when undertaking a trip from Paris to Milan. On 4 May 1949, Catella was testing a G46, a light monoplane used only for training purposes. Flying at approximately 500 metres above the ground, he noticed that the hill of Superga was clearly visible below the dark grey clouds. Seeking permission to land from the control tower at Aeritalia, Catella inadvertently made contact with another aircraft. It was the plane carrying the Torino players back home, under the control of Pierluigi Meroni.

During their conversation, Meroni told Catella that he had just flown over the Apennines below the clouds and that he was flying 'at sight' without any problems.

In good spirits, Meroni said that he would be landing at the Aeritalia airfield in approximately 20 minutes and asked Catella to prepare a coffee for him. On landing his own aircraft, Catella recalled his conversation with Meroni and made the drink for his friend. Then he heard a telephone ringing. It was a communication from the control tower saying that a plane had just crashed against the church of Superga. Realising that there was only one aircraft flying in the area that afternoon, Catella was overcome by a feeling of disbelief. Although he could not bring himself to admit it, he knew it was the Torino plane.

Vittore Catella and a journalist from *La Stampa* were among the first people to reach the scene at Superga. Arriving at the site of the church they were directed by the few carabinieri present to where a tragedy had occurred. There, just a few metres away, they saw scattered across scorched fields the twisted fragments of the aircraft and some bodies. The corpses were badly mutilated but in the carnage Catella could make out the silent figure of Valentino Mazzola whose face was still intact and looking towards the sky.

Minutes later, others started to arrive. They included Ferruccio Novo and Sauro Toma, who, both in a state of shock, were unable to comprehend the situation around them. Toma was crying, praying that at any moment he would wake up from the nightmare confronting him. Because his injury he had been unable to travel with his teammates but now he was alive while all his friends were dead. It was a bitter twist of fate. By now many more people had appeared at the site as the rain still poured down on the wreckage and the bodies. Toma was also able to identify the body of Mazzola but at that point the secretary of Torino, Giusti, came across and led Toma away from the scene.

The Juventus president, Giovanni Agnelli, together with his club's players John Hansen and Teobaldo Depetrini, also arrived to the scene and were soon joined by the relatives of the victims as news of the tragedy began to unfold. The immediate task of identifying the players was assigned to Vittorio Pozzo who, as national coach, knew them all well. The process was slow and painful as the majority of the bodies were badly mutilated and unrecognisable from the great athletes that Pozzo had loved and admired so much. Most of the victims could be identified only by searching through their documents and personal belongings. For instance, Aldo Ballarin was recognised by the pass - port found in his trouser pocket, and Mario Rigamonti from the ring he was wearing. An envelope containing postage stamps gave the clue to the body of Ruggero Grava, well known as an avid philatelist. Slowly the identification of the players continued.

The aftermath of the crash

As an experienced pilot, Vittore Catella was quick to suggest that the accident could not have been caused by any technical fault with the aircraft. He argued that it was unlikely there had been an engine block or a malfunction of the altimeter, as there were at least four of these in the plane which in an emergency situation could be regulated by hand. Also, the aircraft had only recently been built and was considered to be 'state of the art'. Catella believed the tragedy was due to human error and that if the plane had flown just metres away from the church, the crash would never have happened. As it was raining hard that day, the clouds were higher than normal, meaning that Meroni most probably made the decision to fly below them to navigate by sight. Catella believed that when Meroni arrived close to the hill of Superga, he must have seen the outline of the church in the distance. The plane was flying at approximately 270 kilometres per hour, and at a height of between 50 and 200 metres, due to the heavy clouds which covered the hill. The problem would not have been one of altitude but of having to pass around the church of Superga while maintaining sufficient distance from it.

That afternoon Meroni decided to use the church, which was situated at the summit of the hill, as a reference point and pass around it as he had done on many previous flights in the area. It was likely that the church of Superga was to the left of Meroni's flight path, meaning that by maintaining his course he would have been able to clear the hill sufficiently to reduce engine power and prepare for landing. At the last minute, clouds may have obstructed the pilot's view which, combined with the heavy rain, caused him to lose control and as a consequence a wing of the plane hit the ground. The impact was so strong that the wing became detached from the rest of the aircraft containing the passengers and crew, sending the bulk of the plane crashing into the embankment wall situated behind the church. The collision happened so quickly that the passengers would have died instantly. Catella argued that if the clouds had been lower, Meroni would have flown above them, alleviating the need to use the church as his reference point. By taking this action, Meroni would have plotted a different course and flown over the town of Moncalieri instead. Following this route would have taken longer to land at the Aeritalia field though. But it would have been a much safer option and one that would have altered the history of the Torino club.

Speculation of the crash – could it have been a mistake?

Like any tragedy of such magnitude, many theories abound about the cause of the Superga disaster. The flight record log, or 'black box', did not exist on aircraft at the time so it will never be known for certain what the pilot's last words or actions were prior to the crash. One point which remained puzzling, though, was why, after having received warning of such awful weather conditions over Turin, did Meroni not opt to land instead at the Malpensa airport in Milan?

In the wake of World War Two, the new Caselle airport was under construction in the city of Turin. The airport was part of a massive rebuilding programme being undertaken, aimed at restoring essential amenities and services which had been damaged or destroyed in the war. Due to the priority of the new airport, the Aeritalia site had not been improved and remained fundamentally a military airfield. The nearest airport to Turin already in use was Malpensa, situated on the outskirts of Milan. Why, then, was it not suggested to Meroni that under the circumstances it would have been better to land at Malpensa? The pilot's decision may have been based on the fact that he was confident in his knowledge of the area, especially as he knew that other planes had landed safely in Turin that day despite the bad weather conditions. Or could it have been, as was suggested, that he desperately needed to land at the Aeritalia field in Turin, even though he could have chosen to divert to Milan?

At the time much speculation centred around this decision. It was rumoured that someone on the plane could have been transporting an illegal baggage that could only be unloaded at Turin due to the virtually non-existent customs check at the Aeritalia field. If this was the case, then who transported such a prohibited item? In the resulting search of the plane's fragments and bodies of the victims, such an item was never found. Neither was there any mention of any suspicious package in the official investigation into the crash. So, could any item have been traced that would have pointed the finger of accusation and placed prominent individuals into a position of compromise?

Some rumours circulated about Vittorio Pozzo, the national coach, one of the first people to arrive at the scene and who was given the task of identifying the bodies of the players, ahead of Ferruccio Novo. Added to the intrigue was the reported suicide, shortly afterwards, of the owner of a well-known, prestigious cafe situated in the city centre of Turin. The death was immediately linked to the tragedy of Superga and for months afterwards theories abounded around the city. The authorities who carried out the enquiry have always denied that any items of a suspicious nature were found, or that any individuals could have had damaging links to what happened that day. For reasons known only to himself, Vittorio Pozzo was reported to have always avoided talking about the subject, but it could simply have been too upsetting for him to do so. That is entirely understandable. We will also never know if the pilot, Pierluigi Meroni, really believed that he had already flown over the hill of Superga or whether he was trying to fly around the church. To this day the tragedy is shrouded in mystery.

The cry of a city, the funeral 6 May 1949

By 6.30pm on 4 May 1949, news of the crash had spread all over the city of Turin. At 8pm a radio announcement informed a stunned public that the Grande Torino had perished in a terrible accident. The next day saw mourning on an unprecedented scale. Throughout Italy all thoughts were on the city of Turin and its people who were still desperately trying to come to terms with the events of the previous day. Overnight many lives had been shattered. To the families and loved ones of the victims, the loss was insurmountable. For the football fans, who would never again be able to watch their great team, and for the general public of Turin, time had as good as stopped. A great hole had been torn in the city.

In the midst of this great tidal wave of emotion, arrangements were made for the funerals, held almost immediately on 6 May 1949 at the Palazzo Madama situated in Piazza Castello. The 31 coffins, each made of pale maplewood, were lined up in the mortuary chapel inside Palazzo Madama. Around the coffins, the families, friends and colleagues of the victims sat in silence as tributes were read out by a host of people including the Italian authorities, press and club directors. The most moving and passionate speech came deep from the heart of a journalist named Barassi, who directed his every word straight in the direction of the players' coffins as though addressing them personally. Everyone present was moved by Barassi's words and for a moment it seemed to them as if the players were listening too. During his eulogy, Barassi officially proclaimed the Grande Torino squad as champions of Italy and assigned to them their fifth consecutive Scudetto. Acclaiming them all, he called each of them name by name including the directors, journalists and the plane crew, with the last name to be called that of Valentino Mazzola to whom he dedicated a special tribute: "Mazzola is great. Is the greatest in this room, is great like the world in which we live and is inside all our hearts."

Outside the mortuary chapel, a huge crowd waited for the coffins and the ensuing procession to emerge. There were at least 500,000 people filling the streets and surrounding squares of Piazza Castello, the houses in the city emptying as people paid their last respects to the players who over the years had become part of their lives. The coffins were slowly carried out of the chapel, down the staircase to the outside of the building, each one borne on the shoulders of friends and colleagues of the victims. Each was wrapped in the Italian flag, with the exception of Erbstein's and Lievesley's which were decorated with the flags of Hungary and the United Kingdom respectively. The coffin of Mazzola, the great captain of Torino and the Azzurri, was led by Vittorio Pozzo and carried on the shoulders of his contemporaries and former colleagues in the national squad including Baloncieri, Rossetti, Campatelli, Lorenzi and Becattin. The coffin of Maroso, the youngest player to die in the tragedy, was carried by members of the club's youth team who each wore the burgundy shirt of Torino. That of the *Tutto Sport* journalist Renato Casalbore was carried by friends and colleagues who had worked with him and adored him for 30 years.

As the coffins came into view, a deep shiver seemed to run through the thousands standing outside. Young and old wept together with many falling to their knees as, one by one, the coffins were loaded on to lorries for the start of the funeral procession. Leading the cavalcade were the youth teams of Torino and Juventus, dressed in their football kits, followed by representatives from all the other Italian clubs. The northern Italian teams sent all their players to the funeral with the more distant ones being represented by their directors. All of football was united in grief with everyone wanting to be present to pay homage and to say a last farewell to the Grande Torino.

Juventus were due to play a match the following day in Palermo and had asked for the fixture to be postponed, only for their request to be refused by the league. Reluctantly, the players had been told to take the morning train which would have meant them missing the funeral, but to their great relief they were called back by the directors who realised there was another train leaving for Palermo later in the afternoon. Despite the intense rivalry, there was also a great deal of mutual respect between the two Turin clubs and it was only fitting that the Juventus squad were able to attend the funeral.

The procession made its way slowly from Piazza Castello to via Roma where, in front of the Bar Vittoria which Ossola and Gabetto had jointly owned, the lorry transporting their coffins stopped for a few moments. The procession carried on through Piazza San Carlo, Corso Vittorio Emanuele and Piazza Solferino before stopping in via Alfieri where the Torino headquarters were situated. It then carried on further through via XX Settembre and finally to Piazza San Giovanni where, inside the Duomo, a mass was held which went on until 8.15pm. Members of the Italian authorities attended the funeral, with the government represented by the MP Giulio Andreotti, and the Mayor of Turin representing the city. A final mass was conducted at the cemetery in Turin and the following day the coffins of each of the victims were sent to their home towns for private family ceremonies and their final place of rest. Television, as a mass medium, did not exist in those days, meaning that the majority of people who had mourned that day had never seen Torino play. Unconsciously, though, the squad of young men had represented the first signs of life and vitality in a city and country only recently afflicted, like many others, by the ravages of war. For many people it had been a struggle trying to piece together a semblance of optimism after such a dreadful period. With the Superga tragedy part of that spirit and innocence had died forever.

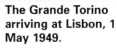

The Grande Torino arriving at Lisbon, 1 May 1949.

Valentino Mazzola (left) and Francisco Ferreira exchanging pennants prior to the testimonial match for the Benfica captain, 3 May 1949, the last match of the Grande Torino.

The church of Superga (circled is the memorial plaque dedicated to the Grande Torino).

Superga, 4 May 1949, the decimated G212 plane of the Grande Torino.

Sequence of the wreckage of the G212 plane, taken just hours after the crash.

Wreckage of the G212 plane

The typewriter of the journalist Rena
Casalbore.

The charred bodies of the Grande Torino players lay beside the wreckage.

The authorities meeting at the crash site.

The national papers break the news of the tragedy.

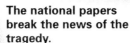

6 May 1949, a distraught Vittorio Pozzo arrives at the funeral.

Two pallbearers from the Torino youth team standing next to the coffin of Virgilio Maroso, the youngest victim of the tragedy.

6 May 1949, the funeral procession enters Piazza San Carlo.

The cavalcade passes through Piazza Castello.

The funeral scene at Palazzo Madama.

Huge crowds gather to pay homage outside the Palazzo Reale in Piazza Castello.

Palazzo Madama. The arrival 750 bouquets of flowers.

The lorry carrying the coffins of Mazzola and Bacigalupo.

MP Giulio Andreotti, holding in his left hand the script of a speech, inside Palazzo Madama.

Supporters gather outside the bar Vittoria, owned by Ossola and Gabetto, on the day of the funeral.

A vase of flowers decorates the table of the empty changing-room at the Filadelfia after the tragedy.

The boot room of the Filadelfia.

Boys asked to be men. The Torino youth team which disputed the final four league matches of the 1948-49 season. From left to right (standing): Motto, Macchi, Giuliano, Balbiano, Mari, Lusso, Vandone. Sitting: Marchetto, Ferrari, Gianmarino, Francone.

The young players of Sampdoria pin the Scudetto patch on their Torino counterparts to mark the Torino club's fifth successive Scudetto, 1948-49.

The plaque at the church of Superga, marking the exact spot where the plane crashed. Engraved on it are the names of the 31 victims who died on 4 May 1949.

The Dark Years

A FTER the funeral, Turin began to search for some semblance of normality but the tragedy had struck so deep that the grief and mourning around the city went unabated. These feelings were shared throughout the country and it seemed incomprehensible that there were still four league matches left to play. After a series of talks between the authorities and clubs it was decided that the show must go on and that Torino must fulfil their remaining fixtures. With the entire first-team squad wiped out, the only logical way to conclude the matches was to play the youth team. The four clubs which Torino still had to play – Genoa, Palermo, Sampdoria and Fiorentina – were in agreement and announced in unison that they too would replace their first teams in favour of their youth sides.

Amid a huge tidal wave of emotion, Torino prepared to face Genoa on 15 May 1949 at the Filadelfia. As the day of the match dawned, supporters made their way to the stadium, passing along familiar landmarks on way to the ground but still unable to believe that their great team was gone. The packed stadium was united, with a mixture of grief, celebration, solidarity and bewilderment greeting the teams as they slowly emerged up the steps which led to pitch level. It was at this moment that the full impact of the tragedy struck home. This time, when the players in burgundy jerseys entered the arena, there was no Mazzola to lead them. There was no Loik behind him, no Menti, no Gabetto, no Rigamonti nor any of the other great players that had graced the Filadelfia over the past seasons and who had brought so much pleasure to those who had watched them. In their place were 11 fresh faces, their innocence about to be lost forever as they prepared to come of age in the most demanding of circumstances. The intention was for these young men to be groomed as the Torino stars of tomorrow but now their chance had come prematurely.

The team which represented Torino that day was: Vandone, Motto, Mari, Macchi, Ferrari, Lusso, Giuliano, Francone, Marchetto, Gianmarinaro and Balbiano with the number 10 shirt of Mazzola worn by Gianmarinaro who also led the team on to the pitch. Of the 11 players, only one, Luigi Giuliano, had played with the Grande Torino first team, having made four previous appearances that season. For the rest it was a completely new experience to play in front of such a large crowd, particularly one with a huge well of emotion about to explode around the arena. The young Torino players carried this tidal wave of grief with them, a mighty responsibility for such young shoulders. Before kick-off both teams gathered around the centre-circle to pay a last tribute to the dead, the silence spreading throughout the stadium and the entire city. The scene was repeated at every ground up and down the country as the whole nation joined together in remembering those who had perished on the hill of Superga.

As the game got under way, a huge roar went up from the crowd, the noise rising to a crescendo when Marchetto scored the opening goal for Torino. Second-half goals from Gianmarinaro, Lusso and Marchetto again gave a final score of 4-0 to Torino and at the end of a draining afternoon Gianmarinaro stepped forward to receive the Scudetto. The remaining three matches were won, against Palermo 3-0, Sampdoria 3-2 and Fiorentina 2-0 to give a final tally of 60 points, five more than the runners-up, Inter. Torino had won their fifth successive Scudetto but the latest triumph was as empty as each person's heart. The glory of the Grande Torino era was over and with it came an uncertain future.

Novo and his attempt to rebuild another Grande Torino

Ferruccio Novo had seen everything he had so painstakingly built up taken away from him overnight. Feeling like a father orphaned of his beloved children, Novo was a man mixed up in a cocktail of emotions. Outwardly he appeared calm but inside he harboured a tremendous feeling of guilt for not having been on the plane. Driven by this great inner turmoil, Novo felt he owed a debt to his former colleagues and decided to start all over again and rebuild another Grande Torino.

The president's plans were heavily reliant on him receiving support from the club's members, but the dictatorial manner in which he had run the club for many years had also bred many enemies and although he received many promises, help was slow in coming. Many of those around him felt that Novo had deserved to be with the players when the plane crashed, a feeling that, privately, he also held. Before the tragedy he had led the way, making all the decisions regarding the purchasing of players and the organisation within the squad. Now, with events seemingly conspiring against him, he was alone with only his memories and pride as companions. It was the start of a period of gloom for Torino.

Novo set about rebuilding the squad with money from various sources. A sum of 200,000,000 lire came via a loan from the 'Coni organisation' and 50,000,000 lire from the Football Federation but although the loans should have been repaid on a ten-year term they were later written off. A further figure of 16,000,000 lire was raised by an all-star squad of Serie A players named the 'Torino symbol'. The tragedy had touched the hearts of everyone in football with Novo receiving many offers of help from various clubs around the world. After careful consideration, he accepted a proposal from Don Antonio Liberti, president of the Argentinian club River Plate, who brought his side to Turin to play a benefit match against a league representative team in honour of the memory of the Grande Torino. The league team, the 'Torino symbol', comprised the great players of the era including Boniperti, Nyers, Muccinelli, Nordhal, Lorenzi and Hansen and was captained by Pietro Ferraris who had won four Scuddetos with Torino from 1942-48. The match finished in a 2-2 draw with the respect between the two clubs being enhanced by them adopting each others colours for their second shirts, an association which lasted for many years.

Two weeks later, on 8 June 1949, in Buenos Aires, Novo and Silvio Piola accepted an award from Evita Peron, acknowledging the Grande Torino. With a strong conviction that he could build another great team, Novo bought recklessly, neglecting his previous rule of ensuring that players were of the right character and ability. Among the newcomers were Swedish imports Ake Robert Hjalmarsson and Para Bengtsson, and the Argentinian forward Beniamino Santos. Other newcomers included the former Balon boy, Riccardo Carapellese, and goalkeeper Bepi Moro. In addition to the promising youth players Giuliano, Macchi, Gianmarinaro and Motto, these were to form the basis of the new Torino team.

The first post-Superga championship of 1949-50 proved, as expected, to be a difficult one but overall results were promising considering the team had been put together practically overnight. A final league position of sixth place could be seen as a positive step forward, were it not for the fact that the championship was won by Juventus who also completed the double over Torino, winning 3-1 at the Filadelfia and then emerging victorious 4-3 in a thrilling match in the return at the Comunale. Although not unexpected, the Filadelfia defeat was particularly hard as it signalled the first defeat on home soil since 17 January 1943, a run encompassing an astonishing 88 league matches.

The season had started in exciting fashion with a 1-0 win at Venezia being followed by a big 5-1 win over Novara, but the following week defeat at the hands of Sampdoria (4-0) gave the first indication that the new team had a long way to go before being worthy of the one that had gone before. During the season Torino suffered some humiliating away defeats, 4-1 at Padova, 5-2 at Novara, 6-1 at Pro Patria and, worst of all, 7-0 at Milan with some of the players brought into the squad lacking the stomach for a fight. Torino needed players who were ready to throw their heart and soul into the club, but for many the burden of replacing the great names was too much. The good fortune which Novo had enjoyed over the years was beginning to turn and of the two Swedish players, Hjalmarsson picked up a bad injury while Bengtsson was unable to make any real impact. The other import however, Santos, was an outstanding success, finishing as top scorer with 27 goals.

Judgement falters and errors are made

Despite the odds stacked against him, Novo soldiered on, still dreaming of an invincible Torino once again. Repeating the purchasing operation of the previous year, he spent all the money available to him and in the 1950-51 season the club became a revolving door with new players coming and going with bewildering speed. Most of the purchases proved unsuccessful and Hjalmarsson and Bengtsson moved on to France with Moro transferring to Lucchese. The sale of these players brought in 10,000,000 lire, a bad return on the 60,000,000 lire investment which had been made on bringing the players to the club only the previous season.

On top of the financial loss, Novo released to Cagliari the promising youngster Armando Segato who, a few seasons later, would prove to be a great player. There was also confusion on the technical side with coach Roberto Copernico leaving the club, being replaced at first by his assistant Giuseppe Bigogno before he in turn was replaced by Felice Borel. To complete the confusion, Hjalmarsson was brought back from France and then top scorer Santos was sold to Pro Patria. With 14 goals, Santos had again been top scorer in a side quickly beginning to slide down the table. The warning bells were now sounding and two crushing derby defeats to Juventus, 4-1 and 5-1, illustrated the ever-growing gap between the two clubs.

After achieving a final position of 15th, things carried on in much the same vein in 1951-52. By now Toma and Ploeger had been sold and coaches were coming and going almost as regularly as the players. After 28 matches Mario Sperone was fired and was replaced by Oberdan Ussello, a former Torino player of the 1930s, who was assisted by Copernico who returned to the club once more.

Heavy defeats were by now becoming commonplace and during the course of the season humiliations were suffered at the hands of Milan 6-0, Napoli 4-0, Atalanta 5-0 and the champions Juventus 6-0. These were hard times for the Filadelfia faithful and in an attempt to stave off the crisis Novo founded a new organisation called 'Torino Sport' with the aim of stabilising the financial side of the club. Meanwhile, Novo continued to buy new players in an attempt to chase a dream which was by now fading fast. The final blow came during a meeting of club officials in September 1953 when one of the directors, named Carver, accused Novo of conducting the purchase of a player without prior knowledge of the other directors. The allegation was too much to take and Novo, by now a tired and disillusioned man, decided that enough was enough and resigned. News of his resignation was greeted with little acknowledgement, scant reward for all the years of hard work and success that he had brought to the club.

Between 1949 and 1950, Novo had replaced his great friend Pozzo as the technical director of the national team, presiding over nine matches of which five were won. Pozzo never forgave him for accepting the position and although Novo tried to heal the rift that had developed between them, their friendship was never restored. It appeared as though Novo's single-mindedness and desire to succeed had attracted as many enemies as it had admirers. Any attempt to continue a career in football now seemed pointless, for he realised that, in reality, everything had ended on 4 May 1949. Years after the tragedy, Novo still could never forgive himself for not going to Lisbon and he carried this guilt with him right up to his death on 8 April 1974. After Novo's resignation, the running of the club became the responsibility of a committee called ' Comitato di Reggenza', formed by four of the people who had previously helped finance Novo's 'Torino Sport'. Despite the new administration, the club's fortunes did not improve as Italian football was now changing too quickly for Torino to catch up. For the next few seasons a mix of young and established players tried to restore some dignity to the club, but each year the task of trying to regain former glories was proving more difficult. With Torino now very much in decline, the triumvirate of Juventus, Milan and Inter began to share the glory.

Goodbye Filadelfia hello Serie B

Although only five years had passed since the tragedy, the era of the Grande Torino already appeared confined to some long-lost episode in time. As the club continued its uncertain existence the only consolation remaining to the fans was that the team's league places stayed fairly respectable with finishes of tenth in 1952-53 and ninth in 1953-54 and 1954-55. However, any talk about the Scudetto or prestigious victories seemed far fetched and supporters were forced to endure a spell of mediocre results.

Yet in the midst of this depression was the encouraging sign that the team was now at least made up of players of stronger character and temperament who were prepared to put their hearts into the Torino club. In the 1954-55 season a player was brought to the club who, more than anyone, typified the renewed attitude of dedication and sacrifice to the cause. The player's name was Enzo Bearzot and he would go on to play for the club for the next ten years, helping Torino from the dark years of the 1950s to a strong sense of revival in the mid-1960s, before later achieving legendary status as coach of the national team. Bearzot was born on 27 November 1927 at Aiello and joined Torino from the Catania club, having played for three seasons at Inter who were then coached by their former player Lorenzi. With Bearzot leading by example, Torino were able to consolidate, finishing ninth again in 1955-56 before improving in 1956-57 when 12 goals from top scorer Gino Armano helped them to fifth spot in the table, their highest placing since Superga. In the following 1957-58 season Torino underlined their improvement by finishing seventh but as in the past they could only look on enviously as rivals Juventus once more enjoyed a derby double on way to another title success.

Despite the success of Fiorentina, who had won the Scudetto in 1955-56, Milan had started to emerge as a dominant force and had followed their championship win of 1950-51 with further successes in 1954-55, 1956-57 and 1958-59, a season of monumental impact for Torino. Off the field activities were beginning to take their toll with a power struggle seeing a succession of presidents coming and going, with resignation after resignation threatening the very future of the club. Eventually the entire club committee decided to resign, leaving only one person in control, a man called Gay-Lora Totino, although his reign was also short-lived and after only 30 days he was replaced by Mario Rubatto and his business partner Colonna.

During the summer of 1957, Colonna gave up his position and Rubatto became sole president. The businessman found himself in control of a club in a precarious financial situation and decided the only way to resolve the problem was by selling players and obtaining a sponsor for the team. After moving some players on, Rubatto found the club its first ever sponsor, a Turin-based sweet company named Talmone who agreed to become the team's sponsors for the 1958-59 season. Part of the deal was for the letter T to appear on the front of the team shirt and for the team to be called Talmone Torino. Although sponsorship and shirt advertising is considered part and parcel of the modern game, the idea seemed almost revolutionary at the time with the fans claiming Rubatto had sold the club and the memory of the Grande Torino 'down the river'. In spite of the fans' protestations Rubatto was in no position to refuse the offer and went ahead, although the supporters remained defiant by insisting that the T on the shirt stood for Torino and not Talmone.

Thanks to the fresh injection of money from the new backers, Rubatto bought new players including the London-born defender Tony Marchi, a former England 'B' and Tottenham Hotspur player, who was signed from Vicenza and who went on to make 29 appearances that season. Another new arrival was the forward Giuseppe Virgili, nicknamed 'Pecos Bill' after the American comic hero of whom he was a passionate fan. Virgili was a very popular player for Torino with his shooting power likened to that of a gunshot by some of the more imaginative writers.

Initially the new season started well with a 6-1 thrashing of Alessandria but the following week a 3-0 defeat was incurred at Sampdoria. Things started to turn sour on 21 December with a 5-1 defeat at Milan and in the next few weeks Torino suffered the indignity of defeats against Inter 5-0, Spal 3-0, Fiorentina 6-0 and Padova 4-0. With morale shattered, a series of upheavals on the coaching side further wrecked the already fragile confidence behind the scenes. The coach, Federico Allasio, was replaced by Quinto Bertoloni who in turn was replaced by Giacinto Ellena before the club amazingly appointed Imre Senkey as their fourth coach that season. Amid the chaos the team, with Lido Vieri as goalkeeper, began something of a revival which included a sensational 3-2 defeat of Juventus with Virgili scoring all three goals. However the momentum could not be maintained, with successive defeats suffered to Udinese 1-0 and Genoa 3-0 before Torino gained a creditable point in a 3-3 draw against Milan at the Filadelfia.

At the end of the season the Milan team with such star names as Liedolm, Maldini, Schiaffino, Altafini, Grillo and Bean went on to celebrate another championship, while on 7 June 1959, ten years after the Superga disaster, Talmone Torino were condemned to Serie B following a 4-1 defeat against Roma at the Olympic Stadium. In a dismal season only 23 points were won from 34 matches with six victories, 11 draws and 17 defeats adding to 36 goals scored and 72 against. Torino had finished in 17th place, one place above bottom club Triestina, and for the first time since their formation in 1906 found themselves in Serie B.

Another change that the fans had to accept, and one deemed by many as unforgivable, was the decision of Rubatto for the club to abandon the Filadelfia in favour of sharing the Stadio Comunale with Juventus. The decision was prompted by an offer from the Turin city council, through Mayor Peyron, and had its roots in matters more of a financial nature than any footballing interest in the city. The ground-share agreement at the Comunale allowed Torino a contribution of 75,000,000 lire in addition to the 55,000,000 lire the club received from its sponsor Talmone. On paper the deal looked a good one as it gave the club a stronger financial base on which to build for the future, but to older fans especially, it appeared the final nail in the coffin and a severance of links to the great days. With so many victories and great memories witnessed at the Filadelfia over the years, the decision to use the ground purely for training purposes was regarded as sacrilegious. The Filadelfia had its ghosts and to many fans the act was an insult to the memory of the Grande Torino, but in the football world times were changing.

The Torino symbol. A tearful Ferruccio Novo alongside the president of River Plate, Don Antonio Liberti (right), at the Filadelfia stadium, 26 May 1949.

Vittorio Pozzo, former coach of Torino and the national team reflecting on a mixed lifetime in football.

The newly-sponsored Talmone Torino, which disputed the 1958-59 championship. From left to right (standing): Vieri, Grava, Bearzot, Bertolini, Tarabbia, Marchi. Sitting: Armano, Arce, Bonifaci, Piaceri, Farina.

Buenos Aires, 9 June 1949. Evita Peron welcomes Ferruccio Novo and Silvio Piola to Argentina on the occasion to commemorate Superga.

Swinging Sixties

WITH relegation, morale at the club had reached an all-time low. As the team prepared for its debut season in Serie B, supporters weaned on victories against the likes of Juventus, Inter, Roma and Milan, prepared for new adversaries with names such as Sambenedettese, Mantova, Catanzaro and Taranto appearing on the fixture list. With no one quite knowing what to expect, Torino proceeded to dumbfound their critics by winning the Serie B title to make an immediate return to the top flight. After opening the season with a goalless draw at Sambenedettese, they crushed Cagliari 5-0 and from that moment never looked back. The final tally of 51 points and top placing owed much to the 20 goals by Virgili who, along with Carlo Crippa and Giorgio Ferrini, was an ever-present, playing in all 38 league matches. After the traumas of the previous year Torino were at least back to winning ways and were even playing again on their traditional Filadelfia ground, although later they were to revert once more to sharing the Comunale with Juventus, only this time for good. For the last match of the season, against Modena, which was won 3-1, the stadium was packed once more with thousands of Granata fans invading the pitch at the end of the game, carrying the captain, Bearzot, shoulder- high in triumph. The regular line-up for the season was: Soldan, Grava, Cancian, Bearzot, Lancioni, Bonifaci, Ferrini, Mazzero, Virgili, Pellis and Crippa, although not all of them were to remain at the club the following season.

On the return to Serie A in 1960-61, the club appointed as new coach their former Argentinian star Beniamino Santos. He replaced Giacinto Ellena who, together with Imre Senkey, had guided Torino back to the big time. Santos placed a greater emphasis on younger players with the goalkeeper Lido Vieri, Carlo Crippa and Giorgio Ferrini soon joining Bearzot in the limelight. Ferrini, who came from Trieste, was to go on to become one of the club's greatest players during the 1960s and 1970s, his loyalty to Torino earning him almost mythical status among the fans, alongside the likes of Bachman, Janni, Baloncieri and Mazzola. With confidence restored, a difficult first season back in the higher league was safely negotiated and 12th position was achieved, although the departure of Virgilio meant that the team lacked a goalscorer with Danova and Mazzero top scoring with a paltry tally of five goals apiece. Apart from a heavy 5-1 defeat at Padova in November, results were generally very tight with the majority of games low scoring, a fact backed up by the statistics of 34 goals scored against 41 conceded. The lack of goals was reflected in the derby matches with a hard fought 0-0 draw in November and a solitary goal defeat for Torino in the return match in March.

After the huge shock of relegation to Serie B a couple of seasons earlier, a greater order had emerged within the club and its directors where previously a mix of jealousy, apathy and misunderstanding had prevailed. In the 1961-62 season a new president, a man called Luigi Morando, was to head a committee comprising 14 other directors similar in composition to the ones formed previously by Count Marone Cinzano and Ferruccio Novo. Indeed, Novo briefly re-entered the association although his presence was seen as merely symbolic, carrying nowhere near as much influence as in his earlier reign. Eager to improve the side, and to add some star quality, Morando sent one of the committee members, Mario Gerbi, to England to finalise the signing of the exciting Scottish striker Denis Law from Manchester City for the sum of 220,000,000 lire.

Torino had been alerted to Law's talent by Gigi Peronace, an early type of agent and a great expert on British football. Peronace had been instrumental in bringing Welsh international John Charles to Juventus from Leeds United, a move that had proved a great success. A decade later Peronace was to be the innovator of the Anglo-Italian tournament contested between English and Italian sides. To help Law settle, Torino took another British player, the English international centre-forward Joe Baker, for whom they paid 170,000,000 lire to the Scottish club Hibernian. With Santos still at the helm the presence of the two exciting British players was augmented by the experienced Enzo Bearzot as captain, with Lancioni, Ferrini and Rosato providing the backbone of the side. As well as being good friends socially, the two British players complemented each other well on the pitch, giving renewed hope to the fans of a return to the glory days.

Alas, this new-found optimism was dampened a little when the opening fixture, against Sampdoria, was lost 2-0 at the Marassi Stadium and then the following week when Torino could only manage a 3-3 home draw with Vicenza. During the game the two British players showed signs of dissatisfaction with their new football environment, reacting to the provocative strong-arm tactics deployed by the visiting defenders with the Vicenza player Puia complaining of being the object of insults and intimidation from Law, although this appeared negligible in comparison to the treatment handed out to the foreign players.

After a goalless draw with Inter, Torino gained their first victory of the campaign when beating Venezia 4-2 on 13 September 1961, following up the victory with a 1-1 draw at Lecco and a 2-1 win over Bologna. The scene was set for the forthcoming clash with Juventus and for the two British players to have their first taste of the Turin derby. For the match at the Comunale on 1 October 1961, Juventus lined up with their great overseas star John Charles in the unusual role of midfielder to accommodate Bruno Nicole in the side. As the game progressed, Juventus were reduced to ten men when Omar Sivori was dismissed for foul play and then they forsook a golden opportunity to take the lead when Mora missed a penalty. Sensing that the game was there for the taking, Torino grew stronger and, thanks to an astonishing goal from Baker, won the game 1-0. It was the moment for which the Granata fans had been waiting and the wild celebrations lasted well into the next week. After only nine matches Torino were in second position behind Inter in the classifica.

Although the talent of the two new British players could never be questioned, their lifestyle was in contrast to that of Italian footballers, for the British game had a culture of drinking and late nights. They were also the subject of suggestions in some quarters that they 'turned on the style only when they felt like it'. On a particular occasion during a Coppa Italia match against Napoli, Santos appeared unimpressed with the performance of his star forward Law and displayed signs of agitation before substituting him. The continuing clash of lifestyles between that of Law and Baker and their Italian teammates was proving a problem off the field with the two British players perhaps surprised by the strict discipline expected of professional players in Italy. In a country where they could not speak the language, they began to feel isolated.

On 8 February 1962, after spending the evening in a night club, they became involved in a fracas with some Italian paparazzi. Driven off at high speed, Baker's brand new Giulietta sprint car crashed into a lamp-post in lungo Po Diaz. Although Law escaped relatively unscathed, Baker suffered a broken jaw and broken nose and could take no further part in the season. Law continued to play on, but the damage had already been done.

There was still no disputing Law's abilities as a footballer and on occasions his sublime skills hinted to the Turin public that the great times were back. The Juventus boss, Umberto Agnelli, was a big fan of Law and wanted him to cross town, or rather move a few streets given the close proximity of Torino's Filadelfia training ground and the Stadio Comunale, to play for Juventus. When the news broke of Agnelli's interest in their star player, the Torino fans took immediate action. Things developed in earnest after Torino lost the second derby to Juventus, 3-1, on 4 February 1962 with the after-match rumours of Law's possible transfer fuelling the great anger the fans were already feeling having lost the derby match. Despite his off-the-field life, Law was worshipped by the fans who considered it unthinkable for him to switch to Juventus, sentiments which were very much echoed by Law himself who had by now tired of life in Italy and yearned for a return to England.

After receiving confirmation of renewed negotiations between the clubs, a group of fans led by Ginetto Trabaldo, the leader of the Ultra group, Fedelissimi Granata, found out where Law was living and called at his apartment in Corso Alberto Picco. It was about 6am when a bemused Law opened the door still dressed in his pyjamas. The fans waited while he dressed and then called a taxi to take him to the Malpensa airport outside Milan where he boarded a flight to England. As far as the Torino fans were concerned he was far better off back home than at Juventus. As a consequence of their remarkable action, Agnelli had to abandon his idea while Torino signed an agreement with Matt Busby's Manchester United – themselves still reeling from an air disaster, the Munich tragedy of 1958 – for Law to join the Old Trafford club for a then record British fee of £110,000. In a bizarre trail of events Busby had finally got his man, having coveted Law since the player's days as a teenager with Huddersfield Town. Law went on to enjoy a legendary career at Manchester United and in all played 55 times for the Scottish national team for whom he scored a record 30 goals.

The swindle of Arizaga

After his experience with the two British players, president Luigi Morando, tired and disappointed, resigned and was replaced by an insurance broker, Angelo Filippone, who had previously worked for the Torino organisation by helping the club financially. During the summer of 1962 he employed the services of Emil Ostreicher as the new technical manager. Ostreicher brought with him good references and great experience having coached the renowned Budapest club Honved as well as the world-famous Real Madrid. Filippone also helped to introduce a host of new players including Amilcare Ferretti from Fiorentina and another British player, former England international and Aston Villa forward Gerry Hitchens from Inter.

At the same time a string of relatively unknown players were also purchased including the Portuguese Diego Arizaga from Sporting Lisbon. Ostreicher, who was responsible for buying players for the first team, was originally interested in Luis Del Sol from Real Madrid before hearing from the coach of Palermo about the great skills of a player called Arizaga, who the Palermo president, Toto Villardo, was trying to sign. Ostreicher also received a telephone call from Bela Guttmann, whose long career had, among other things, seen him coach the Hungarian national team and who managed Benfica to two European triumphs. Guttmann told Ostreicher to buy Arizaga as he was the best footballer he had ever seen – and to act quickly as Palermo were poised to sign him. Advised by Guttmann that the player would cost only 60,000,000 lire, Ostreicher immediately instructed the club's directors to begin transfer negotiations before the player went to Palermo. As a result Torino bought Diego Arizaga, with Luis Del Sol heading to Juventus instead.

Arizaga arrived at Torino in readiness for the 1962-63 season and, amid great excitement, was introduced to the press and fans at the club's headquarters. However, on seeing the new star for the first time, supporters and journalists alike were shocked to discover that Arizaga was overweight and lacked the physique expected in a footballer. Ostreicher invited the Portuguese player to give a demonstration of his talent, instructing to him 'jump Diego, jump', but the new player appeared so clumsy that everyone began to laugh. Ostreicher explained that the extra weight the player was carrying was due entirely to his inactivity during the summer break. He told the startled onlookers that once pre-season training began the extra pounds would soon disappear. However, when Arizaga was later introduced to Santos on the training ground, the Torino coach was unimpressed and by November, Torino accepted that they had made a huge mistake and Arizaga was given away to Catania on the agreement that Torino would continue to pay his wages. Thus, Arizaga, although never having played for the Torino club, returned to Portugal financially well rewarded. The embarrassment of the Arizaga affair was made worse by losing out on Del Sol, who proved a tremendous acquisition for Juventus for whom he enjoyed a long and successful career.

Enough is enough

Despite the problems of the Morando reign, Torino managed to finish in eighth place in 1962-63 with Hitchens in particular proving a great success, finishing top scorer with 11 goals, a feat which he repeated in 1963-64 when contributing a further nine.

In 1963 another new president was elected, Lucio Orfeo Pianelli, a self-made businessman who was already involved with Torino through his financial contributions to the club. During a directors' meeting, a request was made for more money to be put into the club, at which point Pianelli got to his feet and told the gathering that he was tired of seeing his hard-earned money being wasted, as had happened in the previous few years. Pianelli offered to invest more money in the club, certainly, but this time he wanted to control the use of that finance by leading Torino himself. At this point Angelo Filippone stood up and threatened that if Pianelli became the new president, then he would leave the club completely.

Unmoved by Filippone's remarks, Pianelli said that he was interested in buying the Torino club, but only on certain conditions. Twenty-four hours later he attended a another financial meeting determined to become the new owner of Torino. Nobody at the meeting believed that Pianelli possessed sufficient capital or was capable of managing the club's affairs and they were stunned by the seriousness of his intentions. The following morning, Pianelli studied the financial accounts of the club, realising only then how bad the situation was. With his mind already made up, he took the brave decision to take over the club, convinced that he could make Torino into a successful organisation just as he had done with his own business. With what seemed to many a mix of bravado and arrogance, he announced that he intended to take up the challenge of returning Torino to their great status of the 1940s and the Grande Torino. On 21 February 1963 he became the 21st president in the club's history. Once more the destiny of Torino was in the hands of one man.

A dream called Gigi Meroni

After a year spent stabilising the club's finances, Pianelli began to look to improve fortunes on the pitch. One of his first moves as president was to appoint a new coach, with Santos being replaced by the Milan coach Nereo Rocco. The president wanted to oversee a new Torino, with exciting players once more thrilling the fans, and with the team now under the shrewd guidance of Rocco, optimism was higher than it had been for many years. The following season, 1964-65, Pianelli bought Luigi Simoni from Mantova, and from Genoa he added the unpredictable wing skills of Luigi Meroni to the squad. Born at Como on 24 February 1943, Meroni had made his debut for Genoa as a 19-year-old on 1 November 1962, in a 3-1 defeat against Inter. Meroni was an exciting prospect and a great purchase for the team and although not yet the finished article there was no doubt that he had the talent and skill to become a truly great player. At Genoa he had been the idol of the Curva Nord and on hearing the news of his imminent transfer the Genoa fans showed their disgust at the club's decision by staging a demonstration in the city square.

Pianelli had financed part of the 270,000,000 lire required for the Meroni transfer by selling Joaquim Peiro to Inter. With eight goals the previous season, Peiro had made a useful contribution but with the arrival of the new signings Pianelli and Rocco were looking for greater things.

The team at last began to show promise and ended the season in third place behind Inter and Milan, and three places higher than rivals Juventus who finished sixth. This was the best position achieved by Torino in Serie A since Superga with the team looking as if they were at last on their way back, the delight expressed by the fans being owed in no small part to the performances of Meroni. With both new boy Simoni and the already established Ferrini contributing ten goals apiece, Torino were once more displaying a hint of the renowned attacking prowess of their famed predecessors. With Meroni creating the chances, and dazzling both fans and opponents alike with his fancy footwork and dribbling skills, the future appeared brighter than for many years.

Added to their domestic revival, Torino had also made their debut in Europe that season. Reaching the Final of the Coppa Italia in 1964, they drew lots with their co-Finalists, Roma, to decide who should enter Europe. Torino won that particular lottery but then lost the Final 1-0. Nevertheless, after a fine run which included wins over Fortuna Geleen, Haka Valkeakoski and Dinamo Zagreb reached the semi-final of the Cup-winners' Cup before eventually being defeated by the West German side, Munich

1860 in a play-off game at the neutral ground of Letzigrund in Zurich. Despite missing out on an appearance at Wembley against West Ham United, the international door had been opened once more and the club, team and supporters began to breathe new air.

The sparkling form of Meroni soon drew admiration from other clubs with the mercurial winger becoming the subject of various bids, including one from Juventus who made an offer of 700,000,000 lire to buy him. And on 21 June 1967, Pianelli and his Juventus counterpart Agnelli signed an agreement for Meroni to join Torino's most bitter rivals. As was the case a few years earlier with Denis Law, the fans soon found out about the news and again, under the leadership of Ginetto Trabaldo from the hardcore group Fedelissimi Granata, took immediate action. In an attempt to make him change his mind, the fans went to speak to Pianelli but the president was in no mood to listen, arguing that the money was too good to turn down.

Outraged that Meroni, the symbol of the renewed hope for the club, would end up in the black and white of Juventus, they decided to go to the Filadelfia where a meeting was hastily organised with the other Torino ultra clubs. A leaflet was printed for distribution in the city with the fans' next action being a demonstration under the windows of Agnelli's office where they continued to vent their anger and frustration. They then turned their attention to the prestigious Ambasciatori Hotel situated in the city centre of Turin, where the Torino directors were attending a meeting, and continued their noisy protest. Stunned by the ferocity of the fans' protests, Pianelli and Agnelli decided that the transfer could provoke an outbreak of violence around the city and so decided to cancel the agreement. Fan power had won the day again and Meroni remained a Torino player.

The city cries again

Although a whimsical figure and rather skinny, Luigi Meroni was a strong, courageous player. Off the field he was regarded as something of a rebel with a dissolute attitude and a liking for painting and would often be seen wandering around town in flamboyant clothes. As in London and San Francisco, the mid-1960s were the years of flower power and the hippies in Italy, and Meroni, already an extravagant character, reflected the social change by keeping his hair long and sporting a moustache and sometimes a beard. His appearance, both on and off the field, was not unlike that of another star player of the time, the Irish genius George Best. Like Best, Meroni was viewed as a trendsetter with the two players also sharing an uncanny resemblance on the pitch, particularly in the nonchalant way in which they dribbled past opponents. Meroni's appearance was so unkempt for some that he was denied a place in the national team unless he changed his image.

Meroni's reputation acquired further notoriety when it was discovered that he was living with a married woman, something which at the time was considered almost a crime to those brought up in strict Roman Catholic tradition. With accusing fingers pointing from all directions, Pianelli leapt to his defence, deflecting all criticism of his young star. Eventually, Meroni took heed of opinion and cut his hair shorter for the love of his country, his sacrifice being rewarded with a call up to the national squad for the 1966 World Cup in England. In the tournament, Italy were knocked out in sensational fashion, 1-0 by the minnows of North Korea whose winning goal was scored by a full-time dentist and part-time footballer named Pak Do Ik. The Azzurri had been sent tumbling from the World Cup and the country was so outraged that the squad was greeted with rotten fruit on their arrival back in Italy. The national coach, Edmondo Fabbri, was pilloried by press and fans alike, admitting that one of his biggest mistakes was in not playing Meroni who had not featured in a single match. Instead of becoming a national idol that summer, Meroni could only look on as Pak Do Ik became the most talked about footballer in Italy during 1966.

The post-World Cup season of 1966-67 was to be the last for Torino with Rocco as coach. Roberto Rosato was sold to Milan with Mario Trebbi and the 34-year-old Cesare Maldini moving in the opposite direction. Meroni was teamed up with the Argentinian forward Nestor Combin who had been brought to Italy initially by Juventus. Combin had not enjoyed the best of times at Juventus and had been sold to Varese, but in Torino he found a new home scoring seven goals with Meroni top-scoring with nine. However the season was to prove disappointing with a final placing of seventh leading the fans to turn their disenchantment towards Rocco who duly left the club to return to Milan.

During his four seasons in charge, Torino had finished seventh, third, tenth and seventh in the classifica but the optimism which heralded his arrival had by now faded. Despite becoming a 'public enemy number one' figure after his failure in the World Cup, the former national coach Edmondo Fabbri was given the opportunity by Pianelli to resurrect his career with Torino and in 1967-68 he began building his team around Ferrini, G. Battista Moschino, Vieri, Poletti, Fossati and Meroni.

Despite their concern over Fabbri's appointment, supporters began to dream again when, with Meroni in outstanding form, Torino took seven out of a possible eight points from the first four matches of the 1967-68 season. Good times once again seemed a possibility but fate was to once more cast a huge shadow over the club.

On 15 October 1967, after spending the evening in a city bar celebrating the 4-2 home victory over Sampdoria, Meroni was hit by a car and died instantly. Once more the city was shocked that one of its great players had been taken at such a tender age and for the fans, who had seen Meroni as a symbol for a return to the great days of the Grande Torino, their grief was unbearable. As a tragic coincidence Luigi Meroni had shared the same name as the pilot of the G212 plane that had crashed 18 years earlier. To the fans it seemed as though the Superga curse had returned and another light had been extinguished, possibly for ever.

For the funeral a procession of fans bade their last farewell to the little genius, among them his great teammate Combin who made a promise at Meroni's graveside to dedicate the next fixture to him, which as fate would have it was the derby against Juventus. On the following Sunday, 22 October 1967, Torino beat their old enemy 4-0 in a game that would remain in the hearts of those present forever. For this Torino team the occasion had become the most important match they had played in and for the supporters the most emotional since Superga. Combin kept his promise to his friend Meroni, playing like a man possessed and scoring three goals, with the fourth being scored by the left winger Carelli. All around the Stadio Comunale spectators were crying, the tears of Superga had returned for Meroni.

The shock of Meroni's death was a huge blow to Torino because as well as being much loved as a person, his talent on the field represented a big capital loss. The foreign transfer market had shown plenty of interest with Torino standing to make good business if they had decided to cash in on their prize asset. As the team slowly recovered from the loss of its star player, the season ended well with the winning of the Coppa Italia, but as in 1949 the triumph was clouded with sadness. In the 1968-69 season Pianelli thought he had found the heir to Meroni in a young player from Cremonese named Emiliano Mondonico. Although a good player, Mondonico was not in the same class as Meroni, playing a total of only 14 matches in the 1968-69 and 1969-70 seasons. No one then would have imagined that this modest young player was to become an excellent coach for Torino 30 years later.

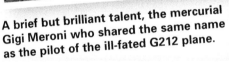

A brief but brilliant talent, the mercurial Gigi Meroni who shared the same name as the pilot of the ill-fated G212 plane.

Dedicate follower fashion. Meroni raised m eyebrow: Italy durii his career with Torii from 1964 until his premature death at th age of 24 i 1968.

The British invasion. The arrival of Denis Law and Joe Baker livened up the 1960-61 season. From left to right (standing): Crippa, Baker, Panetti, Rosato, Ferrini. Sitting: Scesa, Cella, Law, Lancioni, Buzzacchera, Bearzot.

Lawless genius. An idol of the Torino fans, the Scottish star Denis Law.

A Ray of Light
For Torino

AFTER two seasons as coach, Fabbri left the club in the summer of 1969 to take up a position at Bologna. Although Pianelli tried hard to keep him, Fabbri's motives for leaving were personal; Bologna was his home town. One of his last actions before departing the club was to bring a new striker called Paolo Pulici into the squad, a move which was to reap rich dividends for Torino over the coming years. For the 1969-70 season Pianelli made more changes to the squad, selling Lido Vieri to Inter and buying, at some considerable expense, the Napoli player Claudio Sala while also appointing a new coach, Giancarlo Cade. The changes saw only a moderate return – a placing of seventh in the classifica and only 30 points – with the striker Pulici playing 24 league matches in his debut season and failing to find the net in the entire campaign.

The following season proved equally as hard with Pulici managing only three goals in 23 appearances, with the honour of top scorer going to Gianni Bui with a meagre six league goals. Torino ended eighth in the Serie A table but in the Coppa Italia enjoyed greater fortune, reaching the Final against Milan in a match played at Genoa's Marassi Stadium. In keeping with the ultra-defensive style of football that had entered into the Italian psyche, the match ended goalless after 120 minutes and the game went into a penalty shoot-out. Torino held their nerve sufficiently and the Coppa Italia was theirs again much to the rejoicing of the long suffering fans.

During the same season, some supporters had shown a less savoury side which cost the club dear in terms of revenue and reputation.

The first incident stemmed from the fixture against Lazio on 11 October 1970 when the match official Sig Michelotti refused what appeared to be two clear penalties to

Torino and after the match had ended 1-1 he was jostled and manhandled by some Torino fans. A few months later a more sinister incident surrounded the Torino v Vicenza match official Sig Concetto Lo Bello. Torino had led for most of the match but a disputed penalty had given Vicenza a 3-2 win. The fans' anger spilled over when the referee also sent off two Torino players, Fossati and Cereser, and immediately after the match some irate fans decided to follow Sig Lo Bello to the airport, apparently with the intention of assaulting him. In the glare of publicity that followed, Torino were handed a three-match ban from playing games at the Comunale and three 'home' fixtures were disputed on neutral grounds: Torino v Inter at the Bergamo Stadium, Torino v Sampdoria at Novara and Torino v Verona at Piacenza. Although this sort of incident was not uncommon in the football world, the club had been tarnished and for the few fans who bothered to attend the three matches concerned, their reward was paltry with only the 1-0 win over Verona giving any cheer following a goalless draw against Sampdoria and a 2-0 defeat to Inter.

The goal twins Graziani & Pulici

In Italy the changing of the team coach had became a frequent and accepted part of the game and in 1971-72 another new coach, Gustavo Giagnoni, arrived from Mantova, having come to Pianelli's attention after guiding that club to promotion to Serie A. Although he had little coaching experience in Serie A, or of big stadiums like the Comunale, Giagnoni soon gained popularity among supporters when after the first four matches Torino led the classifica.

Defensive tactics had by now taken a vice-like grip on the game in Italy with most matches being won by the odd goal. This was particularly evident in Torino's results but the team now appeared to have a strong mental edge which often enabled draws to be turned into victories. The momentum continued into the new year but on 12 March 1972, during the match against Sampdoria at the Marassi Stadium, the referee Sig Barbaresco failed to allow a goal to Torino after a shot from Agroppi had clearly crossed the line. The match ended 2-1 to Sampdoria and the 'goal that never stood' had cost a valuable point. At the end of the season the referee's mistake proved vital with Torino finishing in second place on 42 points, one point behind the champions Juventus. The outcome was a bitter blow and many fans began to wonder if they would ever see another Scudetto again although the team remained resolute, confident that success would not be long in coming.

For the following season of 1972-73, Torino added another new attacker, Francesco Graziani, to the squad. Before being considered for the first team, though, Graziani needed to gain more experience and was loaned to Arezzo until the end of the season. Although Torino finished a disappointing sixth and managed only 33 league goals, the season saw an important breakthrough for Pulici who, after three seasons in the team, finally struck form, hitting 17 goals, half the team's final tally. Having learned a lot from his spell with Arezzo, Graziani became a regular player for Torino in 1973-74, immediately striking up a lethal partnership with Pulici.

That season Lazio had broken the reign of Juventus, Milan and Inter by winning their first Scudetto, and Torino consolidated their improvement of recent campaigns by finishing fifth with 34 points with Pulici again the top scorer on 14 goals. To the disappointment of supporters, however, coach Giagnoni had walked out on the club in mid-season, signing for Milan following a disagreement over the way certain players had been purchased for Torino. In the event his stay at Milan proved equally as short after personality clashes led to him falling out with several star players.

Torino, to everyone's amazement, now turned to Edmondo Fabbri again and his return to Torino in 1974-75 coincided with the burgeoning of the Pulici-Graziani double act. With 30 goals between them that season the Torino strikers were beginning to build a fearsome reputation as well as attracting a great deal of media attention. Pulici's 18 goals ensured he was top scorer for the third consecutive season, but despite a further 12 from Graziani, Torino could manage only sixth place and had to look on enviously as Juventus celebrated another Scudetto. The experience was to prove valuable, however, as the ghost of the Grande Torino was about to be laid in the most spectacular fashion.

Champions of Italy again

Fabbri's re-appointment had not been well received by supporters and, faced with a regular torrent of criticism, he resigned after only one season. In the summer of 1975, Pianelli employed a new coach who was to become an important name in the history of the Torino club. He was Luigi 'Gigi' Radice, who, as coach of Cagliari, had saved the Sardinian club from relegation to Serie B the previous year. The 40-year-old Radice was a great advocate of modern methods, encouraging the tactic of pressing the opposition and of movement off the ball. In Radice, Pianelli finally believed he had found the right man to give Torino the winning mentality and capture a much dreamed-after Scudetto.

Under the guidance of Gustavo Giagnoni, the squad had made great strides, but in the last two seasons had stagnated with players such as Ferrini, Agroppi and Cerise each coming to the end of a great career with the club. As the 1974-75 season drew to close, Torino already boasted some great players capable of winning the championship – men who included Claudio Sala, Renato Zaccarelli and the strike pairing of Pulici and Graziani – but to improve the side further Radice needed to make changes. Showing there could be no room for sentiment in his plans he released favourites like Agroppi and Cereser and moved Ferrini into a position on the coaching staff after a record breaking 548 appearances for the club. In their place came Patrizio Sala from

Monza and full-back Fabrizio Gorin from Vicenza.

Radice's coaching methods and tactics had been inspired by the hugely successful Dutch side Ajax, who had won the European Cup three years in succession from 1969-71. His new approach saw him establish a strong rapport with the fans who nicknamed him *occhi di ghiaccio* (meaning 'cold eyes'). Torino started the season in disappointing manner, though, with elimination from the Coppa Italia and Europe coupled with an opening 1-0 league defeat at Bologna. However, the seeds of optimism began to grow when, after beating Perugia 3-0 at the Comunale in the second match, Torino embarked on a 15-match unbeaten run which ended on 15 February 1976 against Perugia, who beat them 2-1.

That season Torino won both derby matches, taking the first encounter 2-0 on 7 December 1975 and then, with the season reaching its climax, striking a huge psychological blow with another 2-0 victory on 28 March 1976. At last the fans started to believe their dream was coming true and after a crushing 5-1 win over Radice's old team, Cagliari, on 2 May 1976, the title was virtually in Torino's grasp. Juventus had failed to keep pace and a goalless draw at Verona the following week meant that Torino were champions with one match to spare.

The outburst of emotion and celebration in the city lasted for what seemed an eternity, reaching a climax on the last day of the season, on 16 May against Cesena at the Comunale in a match played in front of 60,000 fans. Radice, ever the perfectionist, was left fuming after his side had stumbled their way to a 1-1 draw but his grimace was removed at the end of the match when he was carried shoulder-high around the pitch by ecstatic players and supporters. Thanks to 21 goals from Pulici, 15 from Graziani, and a mean defence, the championship had been won in style. After 27 long years the Scudetto – and happier days – were back.

Return to Superga

During an entire week between 10-16 May 1976, the city of Turin relived the emotions of Superga, 27 years on from the tragedy. This time, however, it was a party atmosphere which engulfed Turin with the city exploding into a mood of celebration. The impact of the Scudetto success could not be underestimated with a vast number of older fans turning up for the celebrations against Cesena, many of them wearing dark glasses to conceal moist eyes after all the old emotions resurfaced. The Scudetto had brought back incredible memories of the Grande Torino and for many fans a ghost had been laid to rest. As the celebrations continued, the entire city became Granata with burgundy flags and banners draped from nearly every building across the city. The mayor of Turin, who was also a great Torino fan, compared the occasion to the day when the city was liberated from fascism. On the evening of the 17 May 1976, men and women, young and old, and even complete families, started to walk from the city centre to the hill of Superga. Carrying torches and flags, the procession resembled a crusade with the people dedicating the return of the Scudetto to the memory of the great Grande Torino team of 1949. A month later, on 15 June, a grand party took place at the Palazzo Del Lavoro with 1,500 people joining in the celebrations. Torino supporters had experienced much distrust in their club over the years, but on 16 May 1976 they had found their trust again.

A debut in the European Cup

With the Scudetto now won, Torino were at last able to take their place alongside the élite club sides in the European Cup. The competition had started six years after the Superga tragedy and was dominated by Real Madrid for five years after that. For the Torino team of the early 1950s, competing with the cream of Europe had seemed impossible, in another world.

The Grande Torino had been forced to play friendly matches to build on their reputation outside Italy, but now Torino at last had the chance to perform in front of a huge audience with the best clubs Europe had to offer. The competition started well with the elimination of the Swedish champions Malmo, but luck was against Torino in the next round when the draw paired them with the crack West German side, Borussia Monchengladbach. The Germans were experienced European campaigners and proved too strong in the first leg, winning 2-1 at the Stadio Comunale. A stormy goalless draw in the return leg put paid to Torino's hope in the competition, their cause not being helped by ending up with only eight players after the Belgian referee, M Delcourt, had sent-off Caporale, Zaccarelli and Castellini following a series of bad fouls and dissent.

Better progress was made in the league, but after a gigantic struggle with Juventus the positions of the previous season were reversed with the rivals separated by a solitary point come the season's end. One year on from the great celebrations of the previous May, Torino were mere onlookers as the new Juventus of Giovanni Trappatoni accepted the accolades. Amazingly, things repeated themselves in the following 1977-78 season and although at times playing some enterprising football, Torino ended in second place once more as the Trappatoni juggernaut gained momentum.

Over the next few seasons Torino gradually began to fall further behind Juventus and the re-emerging Milan and Inter, the fall from grace being heralded by a drop to fourth place in 1978-79. The following season, 1979-80, saw Torino off to a wretched start and after 19 matches they found themselves fourth from bottom with relegation to Serie B a strong possibility. Faced with the unthinkable, the club managed to haul its way slowly back up the table but a final placing of fourth failed to mask the disappointments of the first part of the season and the first signs of cracks in the club's structure. During that season a scandal had broken out with allegations of 'fixed' bets involving major Italian teams. In April the police and carabinieri had entered the stadium to interrogate players and directors. The clouds eventually passed over but not before Torino had parted company with Radice, who left the club after five seasons as coach.

The saga of the 1980s

In 1980-81, Italian football once again opened the door to foreign players after the 'Veto Andreotti' agreement, which had forbidden clubs to have foreigners in their squads, was revoked. In keeping with the new change of direction, Torino signed the Dutch player Michel Van De Korput from Feyenoord, but despite a bright start to the season they ended up in ninth place in the classifica. In bizarre fashion the club had also missed out in the Coppa Italia, despite reaching the Final against Roma. Both legs had ended 1-1 and with extra-time still not producing a winning goal, the decision was left with the referee who proclaimed Roma the cup winners. By then Pianelli had had enough and resigned after 19 years as president of Torino.

Despite the decline of the previous few seasons, the strike duo of Pulici and Graziani had continued to score regularly but now the partnership had also run its course and at the end of the season, after a tremendous career, Graziani left the club. In 1981-82, with Graziani gone, Torino could muster only 25 league goals with Graziani's successor, Giuseppe Dossena, managing only four. Due mainly to the lack of goals, Torino finished eighth, enduring more disappointment in the Coppa Italia where, after reaching the Final for the second successive season, they were defeated by an Inter side under the guidance of coach Eugenio Bersellini, who would ironically join Torino the following year. As well as the farewell of Orfeo Pianelli, the club bade goodbye that season to one of their all-time great players, Paolo Pulici who, after a club record 134 goals, was transferred to Udinese. With Graziani and Pulici gone, and with the club no longer under the control of Pianelli, it was the end of an era.

Under the new presidency of Sergio Rossi in 1982-83, Torino consolidated by finishing eighth, improving further the following season by ending it in fifth place. One of the stars of the Scudetto that season had been the Brazilian World Cup player Zico, whose magical displays had inspired a modest Udinese side. Suitably impressed by the contribution of the Brazilian, Torino embarked on an ambitious move into the foreign transfer market by purchasing Zico's fellow countryman, and fellow star of the 1982 World Cup, Leo Junior. The 1984-85 season also saw the return as coach of Luigi Radice, and with Junior living up to his big reputation, Torino enjoyed their best season in almost a decade, finishing runners-up to the newly-crowned champions Verona.

For the first time in years Torino had finished above Juventus with their great rivals concentrating on their European Cup campaign where they had reached the Final against Liverpool. For Juventus, the occasion was the biggest in their distinguished history but was to end in the most terrible of circumstances. During an evening beset by crowd problems at the Heysel Stadium in Brussels, 39 supporters died, 32 of them Italians. The match went ahead but with the awful events draining all passion from the game, Juve's 1-0 victory seemed pointless compared to the scenes that had preceded it. Once again Turin had been beset by tragedy.

Top scorer for Torino in 1984-85, with nine goals, had been the young player Aldo Serena, who had spent the season on loan from Inter. Serena had proved a very popular player with Torino's supporters and professed to being a fan of the club himself, so it seemed a natural decision for Torino to make his transfer permanent. However, during the summer of 1985, Inter were keen on doing an exchange deal with Juventus, with the World Cup hero Marco Tardelli moving in the opposite direction to the San Siro. Juventus were still suffering from the shock of Heysel, but their preparations remained as professional as ever and to the great disappointment of Torino supporters, Serena ended up in the black and white shirt stripes.

Under the continuing influence of Junior, Torino finished fourth in 1985-86 but despite the arrivals the following season of Gigi Lentini, Roberto Cravero and Diego Fuser, began another period of decline by finishing ninth. That season the Scudetto had seen an important breakthrough in the monopoly enjoyed by the clubs in northern Italy with Napoli, under the inspired guidance of the Argentinian superstar Diego Maradona, winning the championship for the first time in their history and sending the city of Naples into a state of frenzy. For Torino, though, there was to be no such optimism and after a spell of disappointing results, Sergio Rossi resigned with a new president, Mario Gerbi, elected.

For the next season – and to make way for new arrivals Giorgio Bresciani and Austrian striker Anton Polster – fans' favourites Giuseppe Dossena and Junior were allowed to leave the club, to join Udinese and Pescara respectively. The championship that year marked the arrival of Arrigo Sacchi's Milan as a new force in the Italian game and although a final placing of sixth was achieved by Torino, with Polster contributing nine goals, to many onlookers the team remained unconvincing. As a prelude to a disastrous season the next year, Torino lost out to Juventus in a play-off for a UEFA Cup place, their defeat sealed in a penalty shoot-out. The 1988-89 season saw the purchase of another Brazilian, Luis Antonio Correa da Costa, nicknamed 'Muller' after the West German legend Gerd Muller, but despite his 11 goals and the presence of new goalkeeper, Luca Marchegiani, only 27 points were accumulated and 30 years on from the last relegation of 1958-59 Torino found themselves back in Serie B.

Radice paid the price for the team's failure and was sacked by Gerbi, although the president insisted to the press that the coach had left the club voluntarily. Whatever the circumstance it was a sad and inglorious exit for Radice after the triumph and celebrations he had brought to Torino 13 years earlier. With Radice gone, the former player Claudio Sala took over for a period but neither he nor the third coach appointed that season, Sergio Vatta, could prevent the inevitable slide into the lower league.

A hidden agenda

Like so many of his predecessors, Mario Gerbi had presided over the club with the dream of overseeing a return to the glory days of the Grande Torino, while also enhancing his own reputation. However, relegation had put paid to both ambitions and so Gerbi took the decision to sell the club. Despite the fall from grace there was no shortage of interested parties, among whom were two friends of the director Luciano Moggi, the Blangino brothers Luca and Oscar. The brothers were running a thriving business which on one hand was selling horses for racing competitions while on the other breeding animal livestock for slaughter. Their business experience was reckoned by some to be perfect for the current Torino, although more cynical onlookers simply saw a once-proud club now prepared to sell its soul to the highest bidder. Another interested party was Vittorio Merloni, former president of a large company called Indesit-Ariston, and through Merloni another name entered the frame, that of Felice Colombo the former president of Milan who had previously become embroiled in the fixed bets scandal. The owner of a regional TV station, a man called Mandella, also began to make his voice heard, creating much interest in the ranks of Torino supporters with the romantic notion of appointing Sandro Mazzola, son of the legendary Valentino, as the new president. However, despite the interest of these high profile individuals, Gerbi decided to sell the club to an unknown businessman, Gianmauro Borsano, and on 2 March 1989 Borsano introduced himself to the press and fans as the new owner, president and self-proclaimed saviour of the Torino club.

In the eyes of Borsano, the new decade was to signal a new chapter in the Torino story, one which under his direction would see the club reclaim its place among the country's élite. First, though, was the not inconsiderable matter of climbing back into Serie A. To accomplish this task another new coach, Eugenio Fascetti, was appointed for the 1989-90 season, with new players such as Roberto Policano and Roberto Mussi brought into the team. Due to the poor financial situation in which the club found itself, the emphasis was once more placed on youth, and promising players like Dino Baggio, Giorgio Venturin, Gianluca Sordo and Benito Carbone were given their chance in the first team squad. Added to the talents of Gianluigi Lentini, Roberto Cravero and Ezio Rossi, the new-look Torino proved too strong for the rest of Serie B, winning the championship with 53 points on their way to securing an immediate return to the top flight. 'Muller' repeated his feat of the previous season by finishing top scorer again, with 11 goals, and the final goals-for tally of 63 was regarded by fans as a relative bonanza in comparison to previous seasons.

With the hopes of the faithful restored, the club appointed another new coach in readiness for the challenge of Serie A football once more. This time they turned to a former bit-part player of the late 1960s, Emiliano Mondonico, to lead the new adventure. Although a modest player, Mondonico had forged a reputation as an astute coach and soon wasted no time in convincing Borsano of the need to buy new players if the team was to make any impact among the higher echelons of Serie A. An important purchase was the arrival from Juventus of the defender Pasquale Bruno, whose abrasive style of play quickly acquired icon status with Torino supporters. Along with another new arrival, Enrico Annoni, Bruno quickly became the backbone of the side with his previous affiliation with Juventus soon forgotten. To complement the uncompromising streak in the side, the club purchased the Spanish star Martin Vasquez from Real Madrid, a talented and skillful playmaker who had built a growing reputation around Europe with Real and the Spanish national team. With a squad considerably stronger than that of previous seasons, the Torino club looked forward to a revival in 1990-91.

Gigi Radice is carried shoulder high as Torino celebrate a long awaited Scudetto success, 27 years after Superga.

ino, 1975-76 Serie A champions.

A man with a hidden agenda. Gianmauro Borsano (right), the new president of Torino pictured in 1991.

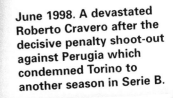

June 1998. A devastated Roberto Cravero after the decisive penalty shoot-out against Perugia which condemned Torino to another season in Serie B.

Francesco Graziani and Paolo Pulici – the goal twins.

An Unwanted Home

IGH expectations for the fortunes of the Torino club on the pitch were not endorsed by events off the field. The summer months had seen football in Italy reach a huge global audience thanks to the success of the country in staging the Italia '90 World Cup competition. To host the event in a manner befitting what is arguably the world's premier sporting competition – some may argue for the Olympic Games – a number of stadiums had either been considerably updated – like the San Siro in Milan and the newly-named Luigi Ferraris Stadium in Genoa – or built from scratch specifically to host the prestigious money-spinning group and final stage matches. With Turin a hotbed of soccer and with its place in the game's history assured, it was only natural that it be chosen as a host city. Yet the Comunale was outdated, too old for modern top-class football, and with the Filadelfia effectively reduced to little more than a memory, the only way for Turin to be chosen as a host city for the finals would be if a new stadium was built.

Consequently – and at huge expense – a new stadium was erected in the Vallette area on the outskirts of Turin. And not only would it host World Cup matches, it would also be the new home of Torino and Juventus who would enter into a ground-sharing agreement in the 71,000 capacity venue. The new stadium was called the Delle Alpi, taking its name from the nearby Alps, but despite playing host to Brazil and the semi-final between England and West Germany, the ground soon proved unpopular with spectators who complained that the large running track separating players from fans ruined the atmosphere.

Another problem was that the decision to share the new ground had been taken by the clubs before the cost of erecting it began to spiral. The ground had in effect been commissioned by its owners, the Turin city council, who entered into a contract allowing the company that built it, Acqua Marcia, to take threequarters of stadium's advertising revenue. The final cost of building amounted to around 180 billion lire, three times the original estimate. For the council to recoup some of its losses, a huge rent awaited its new tenants. Torino and Juventus had entered into the idea of sharing a new super stadium with open arms but now the arrangement had turned into a financial millstone around their necks.

Against this backdrop of controversy over their new home Torino nevertheless enjoyed a good first season there, finishing in fifth position thanks to some fine wins including successes over Bari 4-0, Bologna 4-1, Genoa 5-2, and 2-1 against Juventus in the derby. That year, for the first time in their history, the Scudetto had gone to the Sampdoria of Vialli, Mancini and the former Torino player Dossena, with their success, following that of recent winners Napoli, an important breakthrough against the monopoly enjoyed by the big three of Juventus, Milan and Inter. Sampdoria's success had once more given hope to the chasing pack of clubs, of which Torino were now again part. Fifth place had opened the doors to European competition and with it the financial possibilities that a good run would bring.

As far as Torino were concerned the first season at the Delle Alpi could be hailed a resounding success. The fans, and in particular the hardcore ultra groups like the Ultra Granata, had adapted quickly with the Curva Nord end of the stadium becoming the new home of the Curva Maratona, with the most fanatical Torino supporters taking up residence among the three huge tiers of seating in the area directly behind the goal. With the club back in Europe, supporters could now look forward to putting on the type of colourful choreography that had once made them one of the best fan groups in Italy.

To strengthen the team for the European campaign of 1991-92, Belgium World Cup player Vincenzo Scifo was signed from the French club Auxerre. Scifo had played for Inter a few seasons earlier and Torino had to fight off strong opposition from them to bring the player to Turin. Another new arrival was the Brazilian striker Walter Casagrande from Ascoli, and with the team now considerably stronger on all fronts, Torino looked better placed than at any time since the Scudetto period of the mid-1970s to capture some long-awaited silverware. During the season, two more players from the youth team were added to the first-team squad, one of whom, Christian Vieri, would later become a star of the national team and command a world record transfer fee.

For once Torino lived up to expectations, enjoying a fine Serie A campaign in finishing third behind Capello's new Milan side which contained the great Dutch trio of Gullit, Rijkaard and Van Basten. In the UEFA Cup, Torino also went from strength to strength, progressing past FF Reykjavik, Boavista, AEK Athens and Boldklubben 1903 to set up a mouth-watering semi-final against the past masters of Europe, Real Madrid. After Torino's 2-1 defeat in Madrid, the Delle Alpi prepared for one of the great nights in the return leg, and in an electric atmosphere reminiscent of the great days of the Grande Torino the team responded with a stirring display to gain a memorable 2-0 win and a place in the UEFA Cup Final. The atmosphere created inside the stadium was taken to another level in the first leg of the Final against the Dutch aristocrats Ajax with the sides playing out a thrilling 2-2 draw. Yet with the loss of the all-important away goals, the task appeared too great for Torino in Amsterdam, their fate sealed by the width of the crossbar which kept out a volley from Casagrande and which ensured that the match ended goalless. Despite a great European adventure, there was still no tangible reward. Silverware had to wait for at least another season.

A political scandal

After many false dawns, and encouraged by the results of the previous two seasons, Torino officials and fans alike became hopeful of even greater success in 1992-93. Heading this new wave of optimism was president Gianmauro Borsano, who decided to enter the world of politics. Other clubs in Italy had benefited greatly through the powerful influence of their presidents, both on a local and national scale. Both Gianni Agnelli at Juventus and Silvio Berlusconi at Milan had been the major power players behind their clubs' hugely successful enterprises and it had long been recognised in Italy that football clubs were regarded by some as a vehicle for achieving personal and political advancement.

Borsano set wheels in motion for what was promised to be a vital development for the club by organising a political campaign under the Torino name. To launch this he used the best method available to him, that of appealing directly to the hearts of the people he hoped to represent. Armed with a microphone, Borsano began roaming the Delle Alpi pitch on match days preaching to all and sundry of the genuine love he and his family had for Torino, even on one occasion claiming, quite ludicrously, that his dog was a fan too. His actions, coupled with an announcement that he had married at the church of Superga, had the desired effect. Torino supporters, convinced their club was on the way up again, supported him in their thousands. Borsano claimed his new political agenda was to fight to improve the social, economic and environmental development of the city of Turin and the region of Piedmont. He founded a new local newspaper *La Gazzetta del Piemonte*, creating his own personal media spotlight almost overnight and with it the growing support of the Turin public. As far as the fans were concerned there appeared no reason to doubt his intentions, especially in light of the fact that the team were enjoying a successful spell under his leadership and that he had also brought some star players to the club.

Borsano reached his objective on the night of 6 April 1992 when he was elected as an MP (*Onorevole* in Italian), helped in no small measure by Torino's football supporters. In being elected, Borsano had gained the popularity and credibility which he had desired. But there was also the added benefit that his position as an MP allowed him freedom from any charge of fraud, allegations of which were now raising their heads. Just a few days after he was elected, rumours about Borsano began to circulate around the city, so much so that within weeks the financial situation of the club began to give cause for concern. A few months later, various businesses owned by Borsano declared themselves bankrupt and the daily newspaper which had only recently been set up was closed down, creating unemployment among its startled workforce.

Borsano now told supporters that, with his businesses in trouble, he would be forced to sell players in order to bring more money into the club. Despite the threat of the sale of several stars, he promised fans that he would never sell Gianluigi Lentini, the player who had emerged from the youth ranks to become the new symbol for the future of Torino. Such a player would never be sold either to Milan or Juventus said Borsano. A few days later Lentini was transferred to Milan, allowing Borsano to cash in to the tune of a reported 24 billion lire. Other players soon followed Lentini out of the club: Benedetti to Roma, Bresciani to Cagliari, Policano to Napoli and Cravero to Lazio. As a result of the transfers, Borsano raised around 40 billion lire but supporters, now stirred by a strong sense of anger at what was happening to their club, were seeking answers to the questions that everyone in Turin had been asking. The main question was, of course, where was all the money going?

The scandal centred mainly around the sale of Lentini, who claimed that he had never asked to leave the club and that the only reason for his departure had been money. Lentini's comments contrasted sharply to Borsano's stance. He insisted that the player had demanded a move to Milan. Another controversial aspect of the transfer was the confusion over the fee, with neither Borsano nor Milan's Berlusconi appearing to confirm the exact details of the deal. Some people felt that there were tax implications here.

To the Torino supporters, Borsano had sold the club down the river. The Ultra Granata group had still not forgotten the sale of Dino Baggio to Juventus, and this latest series of events convinced them and other supporters that Borsano had betrayed them. With the fans' anger now boiling over, Borsano was forced to leave and for a while Luciano Moggi became the temporary president-manager of the club. With Borsano's name splashed all over the Italian national press and with allegations of fraud surrounding him, the Torino club once more had no option but to look for a new owner.

It's all over again

In February 1993, in the midst of much political turmoil, Torino found a new president in 37-year-old Roberto Goveani, a man who hailed from the small town of Pinerolo situated on the outskirts of Turin. The wheeling and dealing of Borsano had left the club in a bad financial situation and one of the first tasks the new president took on was to arrange a press conference to convey this message to an anxious public. Goveani was keen to go on record to blame Borsano for the present financial plight of the club, citing among other reasons the luxuries Borsano had afforded himself, and the wages given to general director Luciano Moggi and other club officials. Goveani's words created an unbridgeable divide between himself and Moggi, resulting in Moggi immediately leaving the club. He reappeared as general manager of Juventus and a key man in Juve's revival of the mid-1990s. To replace Moggi, Goveani called on former fans' favourite Renato Zaccarelli, counting on that move to restore the trust in the club that supporters by now were clearly beginning to lose.

Without the departed Lentini, Torino began the 1992-93 season in fine form and remained unbeaten in their first nine matches before being defeated 2-1 by Juventus on 22 November. New arrivals such as Andrea Silenzi, Carlos Aguilera and Daniele Fortunato helped stabilise the team after the upheavals of the previous months, but following a dip in form in mid-season Torino had to settle for a final placing of ninth. Now, with their league position consolidated, a fine run followed in the Coppa Italia, resulting in another appearance in the Final against old adversaries Roma.

In the first leg at the Delle Alpi, an impressive Torino display delivered an emphatic 3-0 win, but the wild scenes of celebration appeared premature as the second leg unfolded in the Olympic Stadium. In Rome on 19 June, the home side took the lead only for Andrea Silenzi to equalise fot Torino. Then there was a sensation as Roma hit back to lead 3-1. The aggregate score was now 4-3 to Torino and then Silenzi scored again to make it 3-2 to Roma on the night but 5-3 to Torino overall. The home side battled hard and scored twice more to level the aggregate 5-5. And there it stayed with Torino lifting the cup by virtue of their away goals. The final whistle signalled an emotional relief with no one in the Torino camp seemingly concerned that they had contrived to throw away their three-goal advantage from the first leg. The final aggregate score of 5-5 seemed immaterial in the middle of the celebrations. After the great disappointment of losing out to Ajax the previous season, Mondonico had captured his first trophy for Torino.

Alas, in keeping with the trends of previous decades, Torino failed to build from this promising platform and another period of decline set in. Star players like Martin Vasquez and Scifo were allowed to leave without being adequately replaced, with Christian Vieri also moving on, although his limited appearances in Torino colours had given little hint of his talent to come. Despite a fine contribution from Silenzi, who top scored with 17 league goals, Torino could manage only eighth place the next season and their hopes of another UEFA Cup Final appearance were dashed by Arsenal at Highbury.

The following year saw another change at the top with a new president elected in the form of Gian Marco Calleri, a former president of Lazio. The arrival of Calleri in April 1994 coincided with the sad departure of Mondonico, who had achieved much as coach during what had been often very trying times. The 1994-95 season was to prove another eventful campaign for supporters who were now used to this turbulent existence. The new coach, Rosario Rampanti, lasted just three days before being sensationally replaced by Nedo Sonetti, much to the astonishment of the players who included new arrivals, Ruggiero Rizzitelli, Jocelyn Angloma, Gianluca Pessotto and the Ghanaian player Pele. Rizzitelli proved to be an outstanding success, finishing with 19 goals including doubles in both derby matches against Juventus. Inspired by Gianluca Vialli, Juventus powered their way to their first Scudetto success for nearly ten years but could not prevent Torino completing the double, with victories of 3-2 in November and 2-1 in April.

However, despite the derby successes the season was bitter sweet because while Torino fans could claim to be Turin's top dogs that season, there could be no disputing the re-emergence of Juventus as a major football force. With the Scudetto in the hands of their great rivals, Torino were left to reflect on a final placing of 11th in a season that had, for the first time in the history of Italian football, seen three points awarded for a victory.

Supporters' suffering, though, was nothing compared to what was endured in the following 1995-96 season. Despite a further 11 goals from Rizzitelli, the team gradually lost form, recording only two wins from the opening 11 matches before facing Juventus in the first derby on 3 December. The rapidly developing gulf in class was evidenced by a crushing 5-0 defeat which seriously undermined the confidence of the team and supporters. As the season wore on the slump continued, culminating in a final position of 16th and relegation to Serie B for the third time. At the same time as Torino contemplated another spell in the lower reaches of the Italian game, Juventus captured the Champions Cup. The morale within the Torino club and its supporters had reached a low unparalleled since Superga.

A mistake called Souness

Unlike the two previous occasions when they had found themselves in Serie B, Torino were unable to bounce back at the first attempt. The stiffer competition in the lower division, coupled with a weaker squad, reinforced the message that the club really had hit hard times. The climate had changed for other clubs, too, with Torino finding themselves rubbing shoulders alongside old Serie A rivals such as Genoa and Verona in the quest for promotion. New hope came from Parma in the form of striker Marco Ferrante, but his 13 goals were not enough and Torino ended the season way behind the promotion pack in ninth place. These were dark days with crowds falling well below the 20,000 mark. To fans weaned on better times the prospect of second-rate football against lower opposition on cold wet days at the soulless Delle Alpi was simply too much to take. With the majority of the support staying away and dreaming of better days it was left to the hardcore fans to keep the faith going, although even the Curva Maratona cut a sad and lonely sight on occasions.

Depressed by the state of the club, Calleri decided to sell Torino and yet another new president arrived, this time in the form of Massimo Vidulich. The following 1997-98 season then saw the former Liverpool and Scotland player Graeme Souness appointed as coach in place of Mauro Sandreani. Souness had made his name in Italy a decade earlier, playing with great success alongside Vialli and Roberto Mancini at Sampdoria, but despite enjoying a highly successful spell as manager of Glasgow Rangers he later had a moderate time in charge of Liverpool. Relative success achieved on a shoestring budget at Southampton and later in Turkey with Galatasary had convinced the Torino officials that he was the man to lead them back into Serie A. However, their judgement was to prove flawed after a disastrous start to the season.

The summer months had seen Gigi Lentini return to the club but although still capable of turning in some classy performances, it was clear that he was not the same player that had left five years earlier. Lentini had endured a tough time among the superstars at Milan, failing to fully establish himself in the regular starting line-up and then suffering the trauma of a serious car accident which had left him in a coma and from which he was lucky to escape with his life. To the fans, though, Lentini remained a symbol of the promise shown by the team in the early 1990s and was welcomed back with open arms. The rest of the squad consisted of relatively unknown players who had all been purchased prior to Souness's arrival. One signing made by Souness himself was the Australian-born Tony Dorigo, an England international full-back who had starred for Aston Villa, Chelsea and Leeds before realising a long-standing ambition to play in Italy. Souness had reckoned on Dorigo's experience being invaluable to the side but neither party could possibly have envisaged the part Dorigo would ultimately play come the season's end.

After only six matches Torino looked more like a side heading towards Serie C than Serie A. Heavy defeats against Pescara 3-0, Verona 4-0 and Venezia 4-0 saw the finger of blame being pointed in all directions with accusations of mismanagement at all levels. Souness paid the price for the poor start and was replaced by the former Brescia coach Edoardo Reja who had achieved promotion to Serie A with the Brescia club the previous season. Slowly, under Reja's guidance, results improved and promotion hopes were once more rekindled. With two matches remaining, Torino were neck and neck alongside Perugia in the battle for the fourth promotion place. In the penultimate game of the season hopes were all but dashed after a 2-1 defeat at Perugia, but a 1-0 victory over Lucchese in the last game meant that the two sides had finished level on points, resulting in a play-off match for the fourth promotion slot, an unusual occurrence in Italy where play-offs do not normally play a part in deciding promotion or relegation.

With all club's aspirations – not to mention the hopes of every supporter – depending on the outcome of one match, Lady Luck once again deserted Torino at a time when she was most needed. With every other club in Italy's top two divisions enjoying a hard-earned summer's break, Torino and Perugia fought out a 1-1 draw in the June heat at the neutral Reggio Emilia Stadium. With extra-time still not producing a winner, the outcome was left to the lottery of a penalty shoot-out. With tension rising, players of both sides managed to hold their nerves, but with the score locked at 4-4 the decisive moment came when the unfortunate Tony Dorigo saw his penalty rebound off the post, condemning Torino to another year in Serie B. For Dorigo, inconsolable and slumped on his knees, the agony was a new experience but to Torino and their long-suffering fans it was the continuation of a recurring nightmare. It appeared as if the legacy and heartache of Superga would never go away.

50 Years After Superga

I T IS 2 May 1999, an early Saturday morning in Turin. Any thoughts of lying in are soon forgotten as the first rays of sunlight begin to fill our apartment, a welcome sign that summer is around the corner. As we draw back the shutters, we see below us the constant stream of Fiat cars weaving their way around tram lines, the noise of engines and horns filling the air as people go about their daily business. Although we have only been in the city for two days we are contented to be here, feeling immediately at home with its culture. Although the noise and chaos of the traffic may suggest otherwise, the pace of life is much slower here in Italy than in England with people adhering more to the virtues of tradition and morality.

In Italy, Saturday is traditionally a day to spend shopping and visiting family, leaving Sunday to the religion of football. But today is different, Not only it is a national bank holiday *(festa dei lavoratori)*, the modern demands of television have led to the Torino v Napoli fixture being switched to the unusual kick-off time of 3pm on Saturday. English supporters accept this as a big part of their culture but for an Italian fan this is a break from the tradition of the 4pm Sunday match with which they have grown up. The irony of the situation is that the game is being broadcast live by the new satellite station named Tele +, a sort of Italian equivalent to Sky Sports, and the current sponsors of Juventus. Next season will see more changes with matches being played on different days and times to suit the ever-growing influence of TV sponsorship.

This afternoon's game, although a Serie B fixture, has more meaning than any normal match and will be watched with interest all over Italy. Although two days from the actual date, it effectively marks the 50th anniversary of the Superga aircrash, and to add to the occasion Torino need to take three more vital points on the road to promotion. During our previous visit to Turin last summer, the talk then was all about the return as coach of Emiliano Mondonico, a prodigal son as far as Torino supporters are concerned. The press have hailed the appointment as an assurance of a return to Serie A and to date Mondonico has kept his side of the bargain with Torino, inspired by the goals of Marco Ferrante, in the promotion picture virtually all season. Today marks another important chapter in the club's history, with the past and present becoming intrinsically linked once more. For us, it is a pleasure just to be here and a welcome change to see the team live, rather than the weekly telephone call to Italy or Ceefax update.

Across the road from our apartment is a friendly bar, one of many dotted around the immediate area, where we decide to breakfast. Over cappuccinos and croissants, we play *la schedina*, the Italian national football pool, a few of the fixtures leading us to check a copy of *Tutto Sport* lying on the table next to us. After all, if Lecce are to make us lira bil - lionaires we need to at least check on their current form guide. *Tutto Sport* is a wonder-ful newspaper, a daily journal dedicated purely to sport and mainly football, produced in Turin but sold nationally. There is always heavy coverage of Torino and today is no exception. Most of the journalists favour the Granata as the first team in the city and this morning's headlines urge upon that team the importance of defeating Napoli to begin the commemoration of the 50th anniversary of Superga in suitable style.

We pay for our schedina coupon at the counter and exchange opinions on the coming fixtures with Franco, who turns out to be an Inter supporter and a regular customer of the bar. Although not sharing our Lecce prediction, he offers us an *aperitivo*, such is the warmth and generosity of the Italian man we have just met. We strike up a lively conversation centring around the Torino v Napoli match we are attending later this afternoon and which Franco, like many other neutrals, will be watching on Tele +. As we bid *arriverderci*, he wishes us good luck for a Torino win before inviting himself to visit us in England one day. Before returning to our apartment, we call in at the paper shop next door, run by an old Torino fan, Signor Varta. On sale are a variety of football magazines, one of which is the official Torino publication, called *Ale Toro* which was founded back in 1964. The editor, Piero Dardanello, is also a well-known journalist who for many years was a director of *Tutto Sport*, and his passion for all things Granata has led him to produce a special souvenir edition of the magazine to mark the Superga anniversary, which we purchase although it will have to be read later due to a pressing engagement.

The Delle Alpi Stadium is about a 15-minute drive from our apartment, although our match companions, Doni and Lino, do not share our sense of timing. As arranged, Lino is taking us to the match, but at 2.30pm. his whereabouts are unknown. As we wait anxiously outside he eventually arrives, having stopped for an espresso on way, totally unconcerned that kick-off is less than half an hour away. Being a carabieniere has its advantages, like permitting him to drive at an even higher speed than the average Italian motorist, and before we know it we are within sight of the Delle Alpi. Car parking space at the stadium is plentiful, but as this involves paying over 10,000 lire, Lino decides to park in the nearest space available, which turns out to be a private road!

With time running out, we make our way to one of the many booths to purchase tickets for the Curva Maratona, the area behind the goal populated by the hardcore Torino ultra groups. The best view is from the second tier which is occupied by season ticket holders only, leaving us with the option of the lower or upper tiers. We elect to go for the lower tier which is closer to the pitch and more atmospheric. In Italy, football grounds do not use the turnstile system, preferring instead a final security check by the carabinieri at the gates. After being searched we run down the concrete slope and finally take up our seats among the ranks of the Torino faithful.

The Delle Alpi is a huge stadium with a capacity of 71,000 but today there are vast empty spaces despite a crowd approaching almost 30,000. The gaps in the seats create a cold environment which is underlined by the drabness of the grey surroundings, unlike the colourful arena of the San Siro stadium in Milan. Our panoramic view is interrupted by a continuing series of flares and smoke bombs hurled down on to the track surrounding the pitch by the fans above us in the second tier. Some of the less accurate throws land on the seats in front of us, making the area a hazardous one, although not, apparently, for an ice-cream seller who wanders through the seats totally unmoved by the chaos around him.

As we have arrived late, the game has already started, meaning that we have missed the entrance of the players on the pitch and some of the choreography from the fans. The most vociferous Torino supporters are those above us, with a crescendo of drums banging in tandem to the chants urging on the team. All hopes seem centred on the Torino number-nine, Marco Ferrante, who has his own fan club who drape their 'Club Fedelissimi Marco Ferrante' banner alongside the countless others on display. On the track surrounding the pitch, a big model of a bull's head stands behind a large logo of the club. Either side of it are two huge sheets made by the fans, on the left side is the design of a bull and on the right the emblem of the city of Turin. The sense of history is still recognised by supporters despite some of the younger element who continue to verbally abuse the couple of thousand Napoli fans in the stand to our left. Like Torino, Napoli have also fallen on hard times and it is difficult to believe that only a few years ago the great Diego Maradona was leading them to the Scudetto.

To our dismay Napoli take the lead after only three minutes, scoring at the opposite end to send their small pocket of fans into ecstasy, while silencing the drums above us. An older supporter sitting next to us looks on in dismay, as if he has seen it all before, and buries his head in his hands before muttering a series of expletives in the direction of the team. Happily, his mood, and ours, is transformed shortly before half-time when Torino equalise through the defender Mauro Bonomi. Like Ferrante, Bonomi is a folk hero among the fans, with a never-say-die attitude complemented by a fearsome, aggressive nature on the pitch. His appearance reminds us very much of the present trend, with his shaven head and earring being far removed from the stereotyped appearance of an Italian. Before the smoke from the bombs begins to clear, Torino score again through Ferrante, sending everyone delirious with joy. Maybe this is going to be Torino's year after all. The half-time whistle allows us to catch our breath but Lino, being always on the move, is keen to watch the second period from the third tier where some of his friends are gathered.

Taking the steps to the top of the third tier is not recommended for anyone who suffers from vertigo with the view of the pitch giving the impression of watching the match from a helicopter. The seats around us are all occupied, leaving us no choice but to sit in the gangways with several other fans. Inside Italian stadiums, stewards are non-existent with supporters left to do more or less as they please. Despite the fact we are sitting so high up and the steps are very steep, a little boy, no older than five years old, spends most of the second half running up and down the gangway with no one seemingly concerned over his safety.

As the game restarts, Napoli begin to take control and draw level again much to the disgust of the Torino fans, especially the older ones around us. Unlike the younger supporters, they have experienced better days with the memory of the Grande Torino still inherent in their passion for the club. It seems somehow inconceivable for Torino not to win today, of all days, but deep into stoppage time our prayers are answered when Ferrante rises at the far post to head home the winner, his 23rd goal of the season, to give Torino three desperately needed points. Our mood has turned from dejection to elation in a split second, just like the history of the Torino club. The final whistle sparks a huge celebration of which we are proud to be part.

As we soak up the atmosphere around the stands, spectators begin to make their way to the exits, packing away their treasured banners ready for another day. Outside the stadium a smile has returned, the significance of the afternoon's victory being matched by the beautiful sunny weather.

Tears from heaven 5.05pm, 4 May 1999

Parco Della Tesoriera, between Corso Monte Grappa and Corso Francia, Turin. The spacious rooms of this elegant building are playing host to a fascinating collection of memorabilia. People gaze attentively, pausing to take in every detail of the names, faces and artefacts on display. The men and women are mainly of an older generation, their expressions reflecting as much their own history as that to which they have come to pay homage. The quiet murmur is interrupted by a loud voice which beckons the people to gather outside around the forecourt area. Everyone present follows, for everyone has the same sense of purpose. Once outside, the same voice says a few words of tribute followed by an overwhelming silence. A bugle call then takes the emotion to an unprecedented level. Opposite us, an elderly gentleman, immaculately turned out in a navy blue suit and white overcoat, removes his dark glasses to wipe the tears from his eyes. All around him the same emotion is repeated as we feel our own eyes welling up too. The bugle stops, a split-second silence, then the voice shouts aloud: "Forza Toro, Forza Toro." Exactly 50 years on from the moment of the tragedy we have just paid tribute to a piece of history, one of the greatest football teams the world has ever known, Il Grande Torino.

As the gathering disperses, some go back into the building while others head home or to a bar. We follow the man who has just orchestrated the tribute. Like many of the others present, a Torino Calcio pin badge proudly adorns his smart blue jacket. His name is Sergio Zanetti, a huge fan of Torino and the host of a local weekly TV programme devoted to the Torino Football Club. We offer him our congratulations for such a moving moment. This pleases him and in his strong local Piedmont accent he thanks us for our words, seeming impressed that we have come from England to be present. To Zanetti, Torino is everything. He has followed them all over Italy and Europe. His self-penned Torino football quiz book sits proudly alongside the other books on Toro on the table manned by his wife who is busy selling souvenir posters and postcards. Zanetti fondly remembers the past and the days of the Filadelfia Stadium but is equally keen to reminisce with us over the 1994 UEFA Cup game against Arsenal at Highbury.

His passion for Torino knows no end but others are demanding his attention so we carry on viewing the memorabilia on show. All around are beautifully framed pictures of a very special football team. The faces of these statuesque young men seem frozen into time, in many ways immortal. Although they tell their own story they represent so much more: a city, an era, a feeling. It is impossible to look at the pictures and not read in to them. For the past has become the present and for the Torino Football Club and the city of Turin it always will. Large flags and pennants bearing the Torino crest complement the display, enhancing the faces in the frames. As we make our way to the exit we pass by a magnificent stained-glass picture of Valentino Mazzola, an image which appears immortal and invokes the story of the Grande Torino.

Throughout the day, the sky has been dark with the rain relentless, just like it was on 4 May 1949. Like the tribute we have attended, many more have been taking place around the city, both on an official and personal level, with everyone paying their respects in different ways. Typical of such memories are the ones of an old lady who we encountered earlier in the morning, while sheltering from the rain outside a bar. She asked us for information about a tram timetable and we struck up a conversation with the woman which led to her reminiscing about the tragedy. She remembered that 50 years earlier she was at the dentist and heard a huge explosion coming from the hill of Superga, the noise of which was sufficient to make her jump from the chair. Not knowing what had happened, it was only later in the evening when a radio announcement was made, that she discovered that the noise she had experienced was the aircraft of the Grande Torino crashing into the church.

Soaked through from the rain, we arrive back at our apartment to find the local news station on *Rai Tre* full of coverage of the day's events which have included a memorial service at the Duomo, attended by the officials and players of Torino along with numerous journalists and VIPs, including the Juventus owner Gianni Agnelli. The culmination of the anniversary is a match this evening between Torino and a league representative squad, which despite the awful weather is anticipated to draw a large crowd to the Delle Alpi. After our late show on Saturday we decide to take no chances and book a taxi to the stadium, preferring to spend a few thousand lire rather than risking another coronary. Such is the service, our cab arrives within minutes and we undertake our journey to the stadium in relative luxury. The rain beating down on the windscreens prompts the taxi driver to tell us that the weather is not something unexpected, bearing in mind the date. He tells us, rather eerily, that on every major anniversary of the Grande Torino, the weather conditions in Turin are always the same as 50 years ago. Maybe the rain is representing the tears of the players.

The stars come out

The Delle Alpi seems different tonight. Despite the heavy rain there is a special sense of atmosphere among the fans who are forming large queues for tickets. It is strange to think that tonight's match is basically a friendly because the mood around the stadium is more akin to that of a big league or cup match. We had been hoping to go in the Curva again but by the time of our arrival it is clear that the tickets for this area are completely sold out and we are left to queue for the Tribuna, situated on the halfway line. Tickets for this area are normally much more expensive but tonight prices have been slashed to about 20,000 lire (approximately £7) in an attempt to boost the attendance. The match is a sort of Torino symbol for 1999 and despite the game taking place at a time when the Serie A race is reaching its climax, most of the major stars in Italy have been given permission by their clubs to take part. Taking our seats, the Curva Maratona to our left is a sight to behold. It is a tribute to the loyalty and passion of the fans that they have turned out in such numbers on the most horrible of nights to pay respect to the memory of the team which in essence forms the very core of their club. The noise and colour emanating from behind the goal is something to behold and makes us wonder what would happen if, or when, Torino ever challenge for the major honours again. Various fan groups are represented all around the stadium, with banners of the Leoni della Maratona, Granata Korps and Ultras Granata alongside more obscure ones like The Doors, complete with Jim Morrison image.

For the match, Torino are playing in the 1940s style kit of the Grande Torino, adding to the sense of occasion which by now is mounting as the teams emerge on to the pitch. The feeling of emotion and celebration reminds us of how it must have felt at the Filadelfia for the match against Sampdoria in 1949, when the youth team played in place of the Grande Torino. Cries of "Toro, Toro, Toro" ring out from the stands as players of both sides line up for the photo calls. Guesting for Torino are their former players Christian Vieri and Gianluca Pessotto, whose affiliations with Juventus are briefly forgotten for the evening. For the league representative team, the line-up reads like a football who's who with the likes of Ronaldo, R. Baggio, Weah and Maldini all part of the squad.

The match itself is a low key affair, livened up briefly by the arrival of substitute Filippo Inzaghi for the league team. The Juventus forward is met by a crescendo of catcalls and jeers, with the chant of "*Torino e, e restera Granata*" ringing out, the fans eager to remind Inzaghi that "Turin is, and will always be Granata." The game ends in a tame 1-1 draw which no one is too bothered about. The fact that the game has taken place at all seems of most importance. At the final whistle, as a sign of gratitude to the 40,000 spectators who have turned out, the gates to the pitch are opened allowing the fans to wander freely. Like thousands of others, we make our way down to the perimeter track, pausing to sit on the team bench which, by now, has been vacated by Emiliano Mondonico and the rest of the players. From the pitch, the stadium appears even bigger, giving the impression of being on a huge stage.

To Ferrante and the rest of the current Torino team, it must be a tremendous feeling to play in such an arena and to score in front of the Curva Maratona. Most fans are by now eager to take home a souvenir of the evening and are busy dismantling the goal nets by a variety of means, including a dubious character next to us who produces a flick knife to ensure he gets his momento. The rain, although having now stopped, has left the pitch extremely wet and muddy and in our excitement we fail to notice that our shoes have become a different colour. We decide to walk around the running track. From there, we pass the popular bull's head which is placed behind the goal for each Torino match and see some of the fans folding up the huge banners laid out on the track and which are now completely sodden by the rain and which require several people to carry them away.

With the carabinieri now intent on clearing the pitch we exit the stadium which by now is almost empty. Outside, the crowd has quickly dispersed, leaving only a few diehards who are buying up the remaining souvenir merchandise of the Grande Torino. Being late we take a chance by catching a bus, despite having no ticket and running the risk of an on-the-spot fine. The bus stops about 20 minutes from our apartment, leaving us to walk the cold, empty streets, giving us time to reflect on the evening and what it all meant. It seems that the memory of the Grande Torino is still very much alive, a fact we remind ourselves of as we round the evening off in a pizza restaurant, named appropriately enough on this football day 'Mexico '70'.

A date with the king

Two days later, we find ourselves invited by Sergio Zanetti to another tribute planned at the Parco della Tesoriera, in Corso Francia. This time, the event is taking place in the evening and we have been told that it will include a video of the Grande Torino era. Arriving at the impressive building, which is now used as a registry office, we are met by the sight of several individuals in costume drama. Thinking that they are some part of an amateur dramatics society we offer an admiring glance in their direction before taking the stairs up to a large function room where approximately 50 Torino supporters have gathered. At the front table we see Zanetti, who is seated alongside two other well dressed men sporting Torino ties and blazers. All three are part of a group of fanatical Torino supporters, keen on ensuring that the Grande Torino are honoured in suitable style.

Covering the table is a large flag of the Savoy Royal Family (the former royals of the Piedmont region), who, we are about to find out, are tonight's honoured guests. Zanetti starts off the evening by saying a few words about the history of the building before introducing the audience to the 'King of Savoy', at which point the figure in the wig and gown who we had seen outside earlier, enters the room to polite applause. One by one the rest of the 'Royal Family' are presented, their appearance adding to the grandeur of the evening. The actors, relishing their part in the proceedings, deliver their greetings in a series of speeches. At this point we wonder if the dramatic tendencies of the Italians have, for once, gone too far, but before the evening spirals into a history lesson, Zanetti cuts back to the Grande Torino story.

Originally, the guest of honour for the evening was Sauro Toma, but due to another engagement the former Grande Torino player has been unable to keep the appointment, leaving the audience to a speech which Zanetti delivers in his very strong Piedmont accent. The climax of the evening is a video, which the organisers have arranged to show to the predominantly older audience, many of whom we recognise from two days earlier. After Zanetti introduces the footage with another passionate piece of prose, a power failure leads to the screen going blank, much to the annoyance of the technician who has spent all afternoon rigging the equipment. After a few frantic minutes of reprogramming, the evening is salvaged and the video is up and running once more. The grainy black and white clips of Mazzola and his team stir deep memories for many of those present who greet the end of the film with a spontaneous burst of applause and shouts of "*Forza Toro!, Forza Toro!*" Our journey through time is almost complete, but before we leave, one last poem is read out, written by Giovanni Arpin. It captures perfectly the emotions felt towards a unique group of men.

50 Years After Superga

My Grand Turin

Red like blood

Strong like red wine

I want to remember you, my Grand Turin

In those hard years, you were our only pleasure

Besides war and hungriness we had nothing else

Our brothers had died in Russia and we had to be separated from our family

We lost our flag

We were poor and frightened, the only thing for us left to do was to pray

To enjoy there was little to laugh at

But there you were, Torino, cut from the cloth there was your bravado

All our misfortune was forgotten by seeing you

You were our youth among our hardship

Your face of a working class man, my Valentino, my Castigliano, my Rigamonti, my Loik

and that fussy Gabetto who were sending everyone crazy with your dribbling and goals

Filadelfia! But who will be the villain who dare to call him campo? It was a cot of hope,

life and re-birth

It was dreaming, shouting, it was the moon, the road of our certainty

You won the world, at twenty you had died,

My Grand Turin

My Strong Turin.

Three weeks later Torino clinched promotion back to Serie A with a 4-1 win at Fidelis Andria. The next week, 50,706 fans celebrated at the Delle Alpi against Reggina. Torino lost the match 2-1.

Nel disastro perirono,
oltre ai titolari,
Dino Ballarin
Rubens Fadini
Ruggero Grava
Pietro Operto
Giulio Schubert
Emile Bongiorni;
i dirigenti
Rinaldo Agnissetta
Ippolito Civalleri
il massaggiatore
Ottavio Cortina
il direttore tecnico
Egri Erbstein
il preparatore atletico Leslie Lievesley;
4 membri
dell'equipaggio,
3 giornalisti
(Casalbore, Cavallero e Tosatti) e l'organizzatore
del viaggio Bonaiuti

A city remembers. A souvenir poster of the Grande
Torino 1949-99.

The prodigal son. The return of Emiliano
Mondonico (left) to the club for the 1998-99
season heralded a wave of optimism.

Sauro Toma, the only survivor
from the Grande Torino, pictured
in 1999.

The famous gates at the Filadelfia with
the emblem of the bull, the symbol
of Turin.

Bird's-eye view of the Torino v Napoli game on 2 May 1999.

Curva Maratona at the Delle Alpi Stadium, May 1999.

Exterior view of the Delle Alpi Stadium.

Torino v Napoli, 2 May 1999. A bull's head sits overlooking the pitch and the Torino crest. Either side are two huge banners (left) representing the bull and (right) the emblem of the city of Turin.

4 May 1999. The 50th anniversary of the Superga tragedy was marked by a memorial match between a Torino XI and a league representative side. Pictured wearing the 1940s style kit of the Grande Torino are the starting line-up. From left to right (standing): Vieri, Pastine, Poggi, Mezzano, Lentini. Sitting: Crippa, Bonomi, Sanna, Scienza, Cravero, Pessotto.

ne 1999. Back where we belong. The fans of the Curva Maratona at the Delle Alpi adium celebrate the long-awaited return to Serie A.

Appendices

Torino Calcio – for the Record

League Champions 1927-28, 1942-43, 1945-46
1946-47, 1947-48, 1948-49, 1975-76
Coppa Italia winners 1935-36, 1942-43, 1967-68
1970-71, 1992-93
European Cup quarter-finalists 1976-77
UEFA Cup runners-up 1991-92
European Cup-winners' Cup semi-final 1964-65
Highest points total 65 Serie A 1947-48
Lowest points total 23 Serie A 1958-59
Record home victory 14-0 v Reggiana 1927-28

Record away victory 7-1 v Roma 1947-48
Record home defeat 0-6 v Fiorentina 1958-59
Record away defeat 0-7 v Milan 1949-50
Record appearances Giorgio Ferrini 443 1959-75
Record scorer Paolo Pulici 134 1968-82
Record signing £4 May M to Inter for Vincenzo
Scifo 1991
Record sale £13 M from Milan for Gianluigi
Lentini 1992 (then world record fee)

The Scudetto Years   *1927-28*

North League, Round A

25	Sep	(a)	Genoa	1-2
2	Oct	(h)	Cremonese	2-2
9	Oct	(h)	Pro Vercelli	0-1
30	Oct	(a)	Alessandria	1-3
13	Nov	(h)	Padova	3-1
20	Nov	(a)	Reggina	8-3
27	Nov	(h)	Lazio	3-0
4	Dec	(h)	Brescia	11-0
8	Dec	(a)	Milan	3-1
11	Dec	(a)	Napoli	1-0
18	Dec	(h)	Genoa	2-0
25	Dec	(a)	Cremonese	2-2
8	Jan	(a)	Pro Vercelli	3-0
22	Jan	(h)	Alessandria	4-1
29	Jan	(a)	Padova	4-0
5	Feb	(h)	Reggiana	14-0
12	Feb	(a)	Lazio	2-0
19	Feb	(a)	Brescia	1-3
26	Feb	(h)	Milan	2-0
4	Mar	(h)	Napoli	11-0

Final Round

11	Mar	(a)	Inter	3-1
18	Mar	(h)	Casale	2-1
1	Apr	(a)	Bologna	1-1
29	Apr	(h)	Alessandria	3-3
6	May	(a)	Juventus	4-1
13	May	(a)	Genoa	1-2

17	May	(h)	Milan	3-0
24	Jun	(h)	Inter	3-2
29	Jun	(a)	Casale	3-0
1	Jul	(h)	Juventus	1-2
5	Jul	(h)	Bologna	1-0
8	Jul	(a)	Alessandria	1-2
15	Jul	(h)	Genoa	5-1
22	Jul	(a)	Milan	2-2

	Apps	Goals
Amadesi P.	1	
Bacigalupo M.	10	
Baloncieri	34	31
Bosia	24	
Breviglieri	3	
Carrera S.	2	
Colombari	28	1
Franzoni	25	1
Janni	19	
Libonatti	33	35
Martin II	26	
Martin III	20	
Monti III	24	2
Rossetti I	17	
Rossetti II	33	23
Sperone	28	
Sticco	1	
Vezzani	26	14
Vincenzi	20	1
Own-goals		3

The Scudetto of Il Grande Torino   1942-43

4 Oct	(a)	Ambrosiana	0-1	
11 Oct	(h)	Livorno	1-2	*Loik*
18 Oct	(a)	Juventus	5-2	*Menti 2, Loik, Mazzola, Ferraris II*
25 Oct	(h)	Genoa	3-1	*Ferraris II, Gabetto, Mazzola*
1 Nov	(a)	Roma	4-0	*Menti 2 (1 pen), Gabetto, Ferraris II*
8 Nov	(h)	Fiorentina	5-0	*Ferraris II 3, Gabetto, Mazzola*
15 Nov	(a)	Vicenza	1-0	*Grezar*
22 Nov	(h)	Milan	0-1	
29 Nov	(a)	Venezia	3-0	*Gabetto, Loik, Mazzola*
6 Dec	(h)	Triestina	4-1	*Ferraris II, Loik, Gabetto, og*
13 Dec	(h)	Liguria	3-0	*Grezar, Menti, Loik*
20 Dec	(a)	Atalanta	0-1	
27 Dec	(h)	Lazio	2-2	*Grezar (pen), og*
3 Jan	(a)	Bologna	2-1	*Menti, Gabetto*
10 Jan	(h)	Bari	3-0	*Gabetto 2, Mazzola*
17 Jan	(h)	Ambrosiana	1-3	*Menti*
24 Jan	(a)	Livorno	0-0	
31 Jan	(h)	Juventus	2-0	*Piacentini, Ferraris II*
7 Feb	(a)	Genoa	3-3	*Ferraris II, Loik, Gabetto*
14 Feb	(h)	Roma	4-0	*Ossola 2, Menti, Mazzola*
21 Feb	(a)	Fiorentina	3-2	*Mazzola 2, Ferraris II*
28 Feb	(h)	Vicenza	0-0	
7 Mar	(a)	Milan	0-1	

1942-43, champions of Italy and Coppa Italia winners. From left to right (standing): Piacentini, Mazzola, Gabetto, Loik, Grezar, Gallea, Ferraris. Sitting: Ossola, Osvaldo, Ferrini, Bodoira, Ellena.

14 Mar	(h)	Venezia	3-1	*Gabetto, og 2*
21 Mar	(a)	Triestina	3-2	*Ossola 3*
28 Mar	(a)	Liguria	3-2	*Loik, Ferraris II, Gabetto*
4 Apr	(h)	Atalanta	4-2	*Gabetto, Ferraris II, Loik, Mazzola*
11 Apr	(a)	Lazio	3-2	*Mazzola, Gabetto, Loik*
18 Apr	(h)	Bologna	2-1	*Gabetto, Ossola*
25 Apr	(a)	Bari	1-0	*Mazzola*

La Classifica

	Apps	*Goals*
Baldi	16	
Bodoira	17	
Cassano	15	
Cavalli	13	
Ellena	29	
Ferraris II	30	12
Ferrini O.	23	
Gabetto	26	14
Gallea	15	
Grezar	30	3
Loik	30	9
Mazzola	30	11
Menti	22	8
Ossola	12	6
Piacentini	22	1

			Home			Away			Total					
		P	W	D	L	W	D	L	W	D	L	F	A	Pts
1.	Torino	30	10	2	3	10	2	3	20	4	6	68	31	44
2.	Livorno	30	10	4	1	8	3	4	18	7	5	52	34	43
3.	Juventus	30	10	1	4	6	4	5	16	5	9	75	55	37
4.	Ambrosiana	30	10	1	4	5	3	7	15	4	11	53	38	34
5.	Genoa	30	10	2	3	4	3	8	14	5	11	59	53	33
6.	Bologna	30	8	3	4	4	2	9	12	5	13	53	39	29
6.	Milan	30	7	4	4	3	5	7	10	9	11	39	44	29
6.	Fiorentina	30	10	2	3	2	3	10	12	5	13	55	61	29
9.	Lazio	30	9	4	2	1	4	10	10	8	12	56	59	28
9.	Atalanta	30	8	3	4	3	3	9	11	6	13	34	44	28
9.	Roma	30	8	2	5	4	2	9	12	4	14	36	50	28
12.	Vicenza	30	4	5	6	4	4	7	8	9	13	36	44	25
13.	Triestina	30	4	7	4	1	7	7	5	14	11	32	40	24
14.	Venezia	30	4	6	5	4	2	9	8	8	14	34	46	24
15.	Bari	30	7	5	3	0	5	12	7	10	13	24	38	24
16.	Liguria	30	7	4	4	0	3	12	7	7	12	36	66	21

1944 Alta Italia   The War Championship

(Played as Torino-Fiat)
Liguria-Piedmont round

4 Apr	(h)	Atalanta	4-2	*Gabetto, Ferraris II, Loik, Mazzola*
23 Jan	(a)	Liguria	2-1	*Loik, Ferraris II*
30 Jan	(h)	Cuneo	4-0	*Piola 2, Ferraris II, Loik*
2 Feb	(h)	Asti	6-1	*Mazzola 3, Ferraris II, Ossola, Piola*
6 Feb	(a)	Casale	4-1	*Piola 3, Loik*
13 Feb	(h)	Juventus	5-0	*Gabetto 2, Piola 2, Ferraris II*
20 Feb	(a)	Alessandria	4-0	*Ossola 2, Gabetto, Piola*
27 Feb	(h)	Genoa	7-1	*Gabetto 4, Piola 2, Ferraris II*
5 Mar	(a)	Novara	3-1	*Mazzola, Loik, Ferraris II*
12 Mar	(h)	Biellese	7-1	*Mazzola 2, Ferraris II 2, Piola 2 (1 pen), Gabetto*
19 Mar	(a)	Asti	4-0	*Ferraris II, Ossola, Gabetto, Piola*
26 Mar	(h)	Liguria	3-2	*Gabetto 2, Ossola*
2 Apr	(a)	Cuneo	3-0	*Piola 2, Mazzola*
9 Apr	(h)	Casale	5-4	*Gabetto 2, Mazzola, Ferraris II, Ossola*
16 Apr	(a)	Juventus	0-0	
23 Apr	(h)	Alessandria	7-0	*Mazzola 3, Ferraris II, Gabetto, Piola, og*
30 Apr	(a)	Genoa	4-4	*Loik 2, Gabetto, Ossola*
7 May	(h)	Novara	8-2	*Ferraris II 2, Ossola 2, Loik, Gabetto, Mazzola, Piola*
14 May	(a)	Biellese	2-1	*Ossola, Mazzola*

Semi-Final Round

21	May	(a)	Juventus	1-3	*Loik*
29	May	(h)	Varese	2-1	*Ferraris II, Piola*
4	Jun	(h)	Ambrosiana	6-2	*Piola 3, Ferraris II, Gabetto, Mazzola*
11	Jun	(a)	Varese	6-0	*Ossola 2, Ferraris II, Mazzola, Piola, og*
18	Jun	(h)	Juventus	3-3	*Mazzola 2 (1 pen), Piola*
25	Jun	(a)	Ambrosiana	3-3	*Mazzola 2, Gabetto*

Final round (played at Milan)

16	Jul		Spezia	1-2	*Piola*
20	Jul		Venezia	5-2	*Ossola 2, Mazzola 2, Piola*

	Apps	Goals
Bodoira	7	
Cadario	20	
Cassano	24	
Ellena	23	
Ferraris II	26	17
Ferrini O.	7	
Gabetto	26	16
Gallea	25	
Giammarco	1	
Griffanti	19	
Loik	16	8
Mazzola	25	19
Ossola	24	12
Piacentini	21	
Piola	22	31
Own-goals		2

La Classifica - Liguria-Piedmont round

		P	W	D	L	F	A	Pts
1.	**Torino**	**18**	**16**	**2**	**0**	**78**	**19**	**34**
2.	Juventus	18	11	4	3	44	25	26
3.	Biellese	18	12	0	6	44	22	24
4.	Liguria	18	10	3	5	40	25	23
5.	Genoa	18	9	2	7	34	31	20
6.	Novara	18	8	1	9	28	33	17
7.	Asti	18	5	3	10	21	36	13
8.	Casale	18	4	3	11	21	36	11
9.	Alessandria	18	4	2	12	13	46	10
10.	Cuneo	18	1	0	17	8	46	2

La Classifica - Semi-Final round

1.	**Torino**	6	3	2	1	21	12	8
2.	Juventus	6	3	1	2	15	9	7
3.	Ambrosiana	6	2	2	2	12	13	6
4.	Varese	6	1	1	4	6	20	3

1945-46 Alta Italia

First round

14	Oct	(h)	Juventus	1-2	*Loik*
21	Oct	(h)	Genoa	6-0	*Loik 2 (1 pen), Guaraldo 2, Mazzola, Ossola*
28	Oct	(a)	Sampierdaranese	5-0	*Castigliano 2, Mazzola 2, Ferraris II*
4	Nov	(h)	Venezia	3-1	*Loik, Ferraris II, og*
18	Nov	(h)	Brescia	2-2	*Loik, Ferraris II*
25	Nov	(a)	Modena	3-0	*Mazzola, Ossola, Ferraris II*
2	Dec	(h)	Milan	4-0	*Loik 2 (1 pen), Mazzola 2*
9	Dec	(a)	Vicenza	2-1	*Gabetto, Loik*
16	Dec	(h)	Atalanta	2-0	*Gabetto, Ossola*
23	Dec	(a)	Bologna	2-0	*Gabetto, Ossola*
30	Dec	(h)	Triestina	4-0	*Ossola 2, Gabetto, Ferraris II*
6	Jan	(a)	Inter	1-1	*Loik*
13	Jan	(a)	Andrea Doria	3-2	*Gabetto 2, Ferraris II*
27	Jan	(a)	Genoa	1-0	*Ballarin*
3	Feb	(h)	Sampierdarenese	2-1	*Castigliano, Ferraris II*
10	Feb	(a)	Venezia	1-2	*Loik*
17	Feb	(a)	Brescia	3-1	*Castigliano, Gabetto, Mazzola*

24	Feb	(h)	Modena	1-1	*Gabetto*
3	Mar	(a)	Milan	3-2	*Gabetto, Ossola, og*
10	Mar	(h)	Vicenza	4-0	*Gabetto 2, Castigliano, Ferraris II*
17	Mar	(a)	Atalanta	0-1	
19	Mar	(h)	Juventus	1-0	*Castigliano*
24	Mar	(h)	Bologna	4-0	*Mazzola 2, Loik, Ossola*
31	Mar	(a)	Triestina	1-1	*Gabetto*
7	Apr	(h)	Inter	1-0	*Gabetto*
14	Apr	(h)	Andrea Doria	5-0	*Gabetto 2, Mazzola 2, Ossola*

Final round

28	Apr	(a)	Roma	7-0	*Mazzola 2, Loik, Ossola, Ferraris II, Grezar, Castigliano*
5	May	(h)	Milan	3-0	*Mazzola, Castigliano, Ferraris II*
12	May	(a)	Napoli	2-0	*Gabetto 2*
19	May	(h)	Bari	3-0	*Ossola, Castigliano, Loik*
26	May	(h)	Inter	1-0	*Gabetto*
30	May	(a)	Juventus	0-1	
9	Jun	(a)	Livorno	3-0	*Ferraris II 2, Santagiuliana,*
16	Jun	(h)	Roma	3-2	*Castigliano 2 (1 pen), Grezar*
23	Jun	(a)	Milan	0-2	
30	Jun	(h)	Napoli	7-1	*Castigliano 4, Loik 2, Mazzola*
7	Jul	(a)	Bari	2-1	*Castigliano, og*
14	Jul	(a)	Inter	2-6	*Castigliano, Grezar (pen)*
21	Jul	(h)	Juventus	1-0	*Gabetto*
28	Jul	(h)	Pro Livorno	9-1	*Gabetto 3, Castigliano 2, Loik, Mazzola, Grezar, Ballarin*

	Apps	*Goals*
Bacigalupo V.	40	
Ballarin	39	2
Castigliano	39	19
Ferraris II	38	12
Gabetto	35	22
Grezar	35	4
Guaraldo	11	2
Loik	39	16
Maroso	35	
Mazzola	35	16
Ossola	30	11
Piacentini	10	
Rigamonti M.	36	
Santagiuliana	16	1
Zecca	2	
Own-goals		3

La Classifica - First Round

			Home			Away			Total					
		P	W	D	L	W	D	L	W	D	L	F	A	Pts
1.	Torino	26	11	2	0	8	2	3	19	4	3	65	18	42
2.	Inter	26	10	2	1	7	3	3	17	5	4	52	21	39
3.	Juventus	26	10	3	0	3	6	4	13	9	4	52	23	35
4.	Brescia	26	9	2	2	3	4	6	12	6	8	38	33	30
5.	Milan	26	7	2	4	5	4	4	12	6	8	38	36	30
6.	Bologna	26	8	2	3	3	2	8	11	4	11	30	33	26
7.	Modena	26	6	5	2	2	5	6	8	10	8	24	22	26
8.	Triestina	26	4	3	6	4	4	5	8	7	11	23	32	23
9.	Andrea Doria	26	3	6	4	4	1	8	7	7	12	25	35	21
10.	Atalanta	26	5	4	4	2	3	8	7	7	12	21	28	21
11.	Vicenza	26	6	3	4	2	1	10	8	4	14	28	38	20
12.	Genoa	26	5	2	6	1	5	7	6	7	13	21	46	19
13.	Venezia	26	3	5	5	1	4	8	4	9	13	19	37	17
14.	Sampierdarenese	26	2	4	7	3	1	9	5	5	16	19	53	15

La Classifica - Final Round

			Home			Away			Total					
		P	W	D	L	W	D	L	W	D	L	F	A	Pts
1.	Torino	14	7	0	0	4	0	3	11	0	3	43	14	22
2.	Juventus	14	7	0	0	2	3	2	9	3	2	31	8	21
3.	Milan	14	5	1	1	2	1	4	7	2	5	25	16	16
4.	Inter	14	5	1	1	1	1	5	6	2	6	20	16	14
5.	Napoli	14	4	2	1	1	1	5	5	3	6	19	27	13
6.	Roma	14	4	2	1	0	1	6	4	3	7	16	22	11
7.	Pro Livorno	14	4	1	2	0	1	6	4	2	8	13	35	10
8.	Bari	14	1	2	4	0	1	6	1	3	13	6	35	5

The Grande Torino, 1945-46.

1946-47

22 Sep	(h)	*Triestina*	*1-1*	*Gabetto*
29 Sep	(a)	Lazio	2-1	*Gabetto, Mazzola*
6 Oct	(h)	Sampdoria	1-1	*Mazzola*
13 Oct	(a)	Venezia	0-1	
20 Oct	(h)	Juventus	0-0	
27 Oct	(a)	Roma	3-1	*Ossola, Mazzola, Castigliano*
3 Nov	(a)	Inter	3-1	*Ossola, og, Gabetto*
10 Nov	(h)	Bologna	4-0	*Castigliano, Ossola, Ferraris II, Loik (pen)*
17 Nov	(h)	Brescia	4-0	*Mazzola 2, Grezar, Loik*
24 Nov	(a)	Vicenza	3-0	*Gabetto, Mazzola, Ossola*
8 Dec	(h)	Livorno	3-2	*Mazzola, Gabetto, Castigliano*
15 Dec	(a)	Napoli	2-2	*Gabetto 2*
22 Dec	(h)	Fiorentina	7-2	*Ossola 2, Gabetto, Mazzola, Loik, Grezar, og*
29 Dec	(a)	Atalanta	3-0	*Mazzola 2, Ossola*
5 Jan	(a)	Genoa	3-2	*Ossola, Grezar, Ferraris II*
12 Jan	(h)	Bari	2-1	*Tieghi, Mazzola (pen)*
19 Jan	(a)	Alessandria	0-2	
26 Jan	(a)	Milan	2-1	*Gabetto, Menti*
2 Feb	(h)	Modena	1-1	*Menti*
16 Feb	(a)	Triestina	1-0	*Ossola*
23 Feb	(h)	Lazio	5-1	*Mazzola 3, Gabetto, Menti*
2 Mar	(a)	Sampdoria	1-3	*Menti*
9 Mar	(h)	Venezia	2-0	*Menti (pen), Ferraris II*
16 Mar	(a)	Juventus	1-0	*Gabetto*
23 Mar	(h)	Roma	4-0	*Gabetto 2, Mazzola, Ferraris II*

30 Mar	(h)	Inter	5-2	*Mazzola 2, Gabetto, Menti, Grezar*
6 Apr	(a)	Bologna	1-1	*Loik*
13 Apr	(a)	Brescia	1-0	*Loik*
20 Apr	(h)	Vicenza	6-0	*Mazzola 3, Loik, Ferraris II, Gabetto*
4 May	(a)	Livorno	2-0	*Castigliano, Gabetto*
18 May	(h)	Napoli	2-1	*Castigliano, Ferraris II*
25 May	(a)	Fiorentina	4-0	*Ferraris II, Loik, Castigliano, Mazzola*
1 Jun	(h)	Atalanta	5-3	*Mazzola 3, Loik, Ferraris II*
8 Jun	(h)	Genoa	6-0	*Mazzola 3, Martelli, Loik, Castigliano*
15 Jun	(a)	Bari	0-0	
22 Jun	(h)	Alessandria	4-1	*Ossola 2, Loik 2 (1 pen)*
29 Jun	(h)	Milan	6-2	*Gabetto 3, Ossola, Mazzola, Castigliano*
6 Jul	(a)	Modena	4-2	*Ossola, Loik, Mazzola, Tieghi*

	Apps	Goals
Bacigalupo V.	25	
Ballarin	38	
Castigliano	27	8
Ferraris II	34	8
Gabetto	35	19
Grezar	35	4
Loik	30	12
Maroso	33	
Martelli D.	17	1
Mazzola	38	29
Menti	14	6
Ossola	29	13
Piani	13	
Rigamonti M.	34	
Rosetta	13	
Tieghi	3	2
Own-goals		2

La Classifica

			Home			Away			Total					
		P	W	D	L	W	D	L	W	D	L	F	A	Pts
1.	Torino	38	15	4	0	13	3	3	28	7	3	104	35	63
2.	Juventus	38	15	1	3	7	8	4	22	9	7	83	38	53
3.	Modena	38	13	3	3	8	6	5	21	9	8	45	24	51
4.	Milan	38	10	6	3	9	6	4	19	12	7	75	52	50
5.	Bologna	38	11	5	3	4	4	11	15	9	14	42	41	39
5.	Vicenza	38	10	2	7	6	5	8	16	7	15	53	57	39
7.	Bari	38	11	4	4	5	2	12	16	6	16	33	48	38
8.	Napoli	38	11	7	1	3	2	14	14	9	15	50	59	37
8.	Atalanta	38	8	7	4	3	8	8	11	15	12	40	52	37
10.	Inter	38	9	5	5	4	5	10	13	10	15	59	54	36
10.	Sampdoria	38	10	4	5	4	4	11	14	8	16	56	52	36
10.	Genoa	38	12	4	3	1	6	12	13	10	15	53	53	36
10.	Lazio	38	9	5	5	3	7	9	12	12	14	56	56	36
14.	Alessandria	38	10	5	4	3	4	12	13	9	16	59	60	35
15.	Livorno	38	6	11	2	3	4	12	9	15	14	49	55	33
16.	Roma	38	8	5	6	4	4	11	12	9	17	41	56	33
17.	Fiorentina	38	10	6	3	0	6	12	10	12	16	46	69	32
18.	Brescia	38	7	5	7	3	6	10	10	11	17	45	58	31
19.	Venezia	38	8	3	8	2	4	13	10	7	21	43	66	27
20.	Triestina	38	4	5	10	1	3	15	5	8	25	32	79	18

1947-48

14 Sep	(h)	Napoli	4-0	*Menti, Gabetto, Mazzola, Ferraris II*
21 Sep	(a)	Bari	0-1	
28 Sep	(h)	Lucchese	6-0	*Loik 2, Mazzola, Gabetto, Ballarin, Castigliano*
5 Oct	(a)	Roma	7-1	*Mazzola 3, Fabian 2, Castigliano, Ferraris II*
12 Oct	(h)	Vicenza	2-0	*Mazzola, Fabian*
19 Oct	(a)	Pro Patria	2-0	*Mazzola, Menti*
26 Oct	(h)	Juventus	1-1	*Mazzola*
2 Nov	(a)	Bologna	0-1	
16 Nov	(h)	Salernitana	7-1	*Loik 3, Gabetto, Grezar, Menti, Fabian*
23 Nov	(a)	Sampdoria	1-0	*Menti (pen)*
30 Nov	(a)	Alessandria	2-2	*Mazzola, Menti*
7 Dec	(h)	Inter	5-0	*Menti, Loik, Gabetto, Mazzola, Ferraris II*

21 Dec	(a)	Atalanta	0-1	
28 Dec	(h)	Triestina	6-0	*Menti 2 (1 pen), Loik, Gabetto, Ferraris I,*
Maroso				
1 Jan	(h)	Fiorentina	5-0	*Loik 2, Gabetto, Mazzola, Martelli*
4 Jan	(a)	Lazio	0-0	
11 Jan	(a)	Livorno	3-1	*Martelli 2, Gabetto*
18 Jan	(h)	Genoa	2-1	*Gabetto, Mazzola*
25 Jan	(a)	Milan	2-3	*Menti, Mazzola*
1 Feb	(a)	Modena	3-0	*Gabetto, Fabian, Menti (pen)*
15 Feb	(a)	Napoli	0-0	
22 Feb	(h)	Bari	5-1	*Gabetto 2, Mazzola, Martelli, Fabian*
29 Feb	(a)	Lucchese	2-2	*Mazzola, Grezar*
7 Mar	(h)	Roma	4-1	*Menti, Loik, Martelli, Ossola*
14 Mar	(a)	Vicenza	4-0	*Castigliano, Menti, Loik, Ossola*
21 Mar	(h)	Pro Patria	4-1	*Loik, Grezar, Menti, Ossola*
28 Mar	(a)	Juventus	1-1	*Ossola*
11 Apr	(h)	Bologna	5-1	*Gabetto 3, Mazzola, Ossola*
15 Apr	(a)	Salernitana	4-1	*Gabetto 2, Mazzola, Ossola*
25 Apr	(h)	Sampdoria	3-2	*Gabetto, Martelli, Ossola*
2 May	(h)	Alessandria	10-0	*Loik 3, Fabian 2, Grezar 2, Ossola,*
Mazzola, Gabetto				
6 May	(a)	Inter	1-0	*Mazzola*
9 May	(h)	Atalanta	4-0	*Mazzola 2, Menti, Gabetto*
23 May	(a)	Triestina	0-0	
27 May	(a)	Fiorentina	2-1	*Mazzola, Menti (pen)*
30 May	(h)	Lazio	4-3	*Castigliano 2, Mazzola, Gabetto*
6 Jun	(h)	Livorno	5-2	*Mazzola 2, Martelli, Gabetto, og*

1947-48, champions of Italy. From left to right (standing): Castigliano, Gabetto, Rigamonti, Martelli, Bacigalupo, Loik. Sitting: Menti, Ballarin, Ossola, Grezar, Toma.

13 Jun	(a)	Genoa	2-1	*Castigliano, Gabetto*
20 Jun	(h)	Milan	2-1	*Gabetto, Ossola*
27 Jun	(h)	Modena	5-2	*Martelli 2, Loik, Castigliano, Menti*

	Apps	Goals
Bacigalupo V.	40	
Ballarin	39	1
Castigliano	29	7
Fabian	15	9
Ferraris II	16	3
Gabetto	36	23
Grezar	33	5
Loik	33	16
Maroso	17	1
Martelli D.	27	9
Mazzola	37	25
Menti	38	16
Ossola	17	9
Rigamonti M.	39	
Toma	24	
Own-goals		1

La Classifica

			Home			Away			Total					
		P	W	D	L	W	D	L	W	D	L	F	A	Pts
1.	Torino	40	19	1	0	10	6	4	29	7	4	125	33	65
2.	Milan	40	16	2	2	5	5	10	21	7	12	76	48	49
2.	Juventus	40	12	3	5	7	8	5	19	11	10	74	48	49
2.	Triestina	40	15	5	0	2	10	8	17	15	8	51	42	49
5.	Atalanta	40	14	6	0	2	6	12	16	12	12	48	41	44
5.	Modena	40	14	4	2	2	8	10	16	12	12	45	40	44
7.	Fiorentina	40	15	2	3	3	3	14	18	5	17	49	55	41
8.	Pro Patria	40	14	2	4	3	4	13	17	6	17	65	66	40
8.	Bologna	40	11	8	1	3	4	13	14	12	14	51	52	40
10.	Lazio	40	12	6	2	1	7	12	13	13	14	54	55	39
11.	Bari	40	13	4	3	1	6	13	14	10	16	38	60	38
12.	Inter	40	13	3	4	3	2	15	16	5	19	67	60	37
12.	Genoa	40	12	4	4	3	3	14	15	7	18	68	65	37
14.	Sampdoria	40	11	6	3	2	4	14	13	10	17	68	63	36
14.	Livorno	40	10	9	1	1	5	14	11	14	15	45	62	36
14.	Lucchese	40	10	9	1	2	3	15	12	12	16	46	82	36
17.	Roma	40	9	3	8	4	6	10	13	9	18	54	69	35
18.	Salernitana	40	13	4	3	0	4	16	13	8	19	46	63	34
19.	Alessandria	40	8	8	4	3	1	12	11	9	20	49	75	31
20.	Vicenza	40	9	4	7	1	2	17	10	6	24	31	75	26
21.	Napoli*	40	10	7	3	2	3	15	12	10	18	50	46	34

* relegated to last position

1948-49

19 Sep	(h)	Pro Patria	4-1	*Ossola, Menti (pen), Gabetto, Grezar*
26 Sep	(a)	Atalanta	2-3	*Grezar, Mazzola*
3 Oct	(h)	Roma	4-0	*Gabetto 2, Menti, Ossola*
10 Oct	(a)	Livorno	2-0	*Mazzola, Loik*
17 Oct	(h)	Lucchese	2-1	*Gabetto, Grezar*
24 Oct	(a)	Juventus	2-1	*Ossola, Mazzola*
31 Oct	(h)	Padova	3-1	*Ossola 2, Mazzola*
4 Nov	(a)	Milan	0-1	
7 Nov	(h)	Lazio	1-0	*Mazzola*
14 Nov	(a)	Bologna	2-2	*Mazzola, Giuliano*
21 Nov	(a)	Novara	2-0	*Giuliano, Loik*
28 Nov	(h)	Triestina	1-1	*Mazzola*
5 Dec	(a)	Modena	1-0	*Giuliano*
12 Dec	(h)	Inter	4-2	*Menti 2, Mazzola, Ossola*
19 Dec	(a)	Fiorentina	0-0	
26 Dec	(a)	Genoa	0-3	
29 Dec	(h)	Bari	2-0	*Menti, Ossola*
6 Jan	(a)	Palermo	2-2	*Gabetto, Bongiorni*
9 Jan	(a)	Pro Patria	1-0	*Schubert*
16 Jan	(h)	Atalanta	2-0	*Bongiorni, Rigamonti*

23 Jan	(a)	Roma	2-1	*Mazzola, Gabetto*
27 Jan	(h)	Sampdoria	2-1	*Mazzola, Loik*
30 Jan	(h)	Livorno	1-0	*Mazzola*
6 Feb	(a)	Lucchese	1-1	*Mazzola*
13 Feb	(h)	Juventus	3-1	*Loik 2, Gabetto*
20 Feb	(a)	Padova	4-4	*Menti 2, Ossola, Castigliano*
6 Mar	(h)	Milan	4-1	*Ossola 2, Fadini, Gabetto*
13 Mar	(a)	Lazio	2-2	*Loik 2*
20 Mar	(h)	Bologna	1-0	*Mazzola*
3 Apr	(h)	Novara	4-0	*Loik 2, Mazzola, Ossola*
10 Apr	(a)	Triestina	1-1	*Menti*
17 Apr	(h)	Modena	3-1	*Mazzola, Menti, Ballarin*
24 Apr	(a)	Bari	1-1	*Mazzola*
30 Apr	(a)	Inter*	0-0	
15 May	(h)	Genoa	4-0	*Marchetto 2, Gianmarino, Lusso (pen)*
22 May	(h)	Palermo**	3-0	*Marchetto, Francone, Gianmarino*
29 May	(a)	Sampdoria	3-2	*Marchetto, Audisio, Lusso (pen)*
12 Jun	(h)	Fiorentina	2-0	*Marchetto, Giuliano*

* Last league match played by Il Grande Torino
** Match played at Florence prior to the Italy v Austria International

	Apps	Goals
Audisio*	3	1
Bacigalupo V.	32	
Balbiano	2	
Ballarin	32	1
Bersia*	1	
Biglino*	2	
Bongiorni	8	2
Castigliano	21	1
Fadini	10	1
Ferrari*	3	
Francone*	4	1
Gabetto	34	8
Gandolfi	2	
Gianmarinaro*	4	2
Giuliano	8	4
Grava R.	1	
Grezar	21	3
Loik	28	9
Lusso*	4	2
Macchi*	3	
Marchetto*	4	5
Mari*	4	
Maroso	18	
Martelli D.	28	
Mazzola	30	16
Menti	29	9
Motto*	4	
Operto	11	
Ossola	25	11
Rigamonti M.	31	1
Schubert	5	1
Toma	2	
Vandone*	4	

La Classifica

			Home			Away			Total					
		P	W	D	L	W	D	L	W	D	L	F	A	Pts
1.	Torino	38	18	1	0	7	9	3	25	10	3	78	34	60
2.	Inter	38	12	7	0	10	4	5	22	11	5	85	39	55
3.	Milan	38	15	3	1	6	5	8	21	8	9	83	52	50
4.	Juventus	38	15	3	3	5	5	9	18	8	12	64	47	44
5.	Sampdoria	38	9	7	3	7	2	10	16	9	13	74	63	41
6.	Bologna	38	10	6	3	2	11	6	12	17	9	53	46	41
7.	Genoa	38	13	4	2	1	8	10	14	12	12	51	51	38
8.	Lucchese	38	11	6	2	3	4	12	14	10	14	55	55	38
8.	Triestina	38	11	6	2	2	6	11	13	12	13	59	59	38
8.	Fiorentina	38	12	4	3	3	4	12	15	8	15	51	60	38
11.	Palermo	38	12	4	3	2	4	13	14	8	16	57	58	36
11.	Padova	38	9	6	4	3	6	10	12	12	14	45	64	36
13.	Lazio	38	10	6	3	1	6	12	11	12	15	60	62	34
14.	Roma	38	10	4	5	2	4	13	12	8	18	47	57	32
15.	Atalanta	38	7	5	7	4	4	11	11	9	18	40	58	31
15.	Novara	38	10	5	4	2	2	15	12	7	19	52	74	31
17.	Pro Patria	38	8	3	8	3	5	11	11	8	19	51	61	30
17.	Bari	38	7	6	6	3	4	12	10	10	18	30	50	30
19.	Modena	38	6	7	6	3	4	12	9	11	18	36	49	29
20.	Livorno	38	8	6	5	1	2	16	9	8	21	39	71	26

*Denotes the youth team players who contested the final 4 league matches after Superga.

1975-76

5 Oct	(a)	Bologna	0-1	
12 Oct	(h)	Perugia	3-0	*Pulici 3*
19 Oct	(a)	Ascoli	1-1	*Pulici*
2 Nov	(h)	Inter	2-1	*Pulici, Gorin*
9 Nov	(a)	Sampdoria	0-0	
16 Nov	(h)	Napoli	3-1	*Pulici 2, og*
30 Nov	(a)	Roma	1-1	*Graziani*
7 Dec	(h)	Juventus	2-0	*Graziani, Pulici*
14 Dec	(a)	Milan	2-1	*Zaccarelli, Graziani*
21 Dec	(h)	Como	1-0	*Graziani*
4 Jan	(a)	Fiorentina	1-0	*Graziani*
11 Jan	(h)	Lazio	2-1	*Graziani, Pulici*
18 Jan	(a)	Cagliari	0-0	
25 Jan	(h)	Verona	4-2	*Graziani 2, Zaccarelli, Pulici*
1 Feb	(a)	Cesena	1-1	*Pecci*
8 Feb	(h)	Bologna	3-1	*Pulici 3*
15 Feb	(a)	Perugia	1-2	*Graziani*
22 Feb	(h)	Ascoli	3-1	*Pulici, C. Sala, Graziani*
29 Feb	(a)	Inter	0-1	
7 Mar	(h)	Sampdoria	2-0	*Graziani 2*
14 Mar	(a)	Napoli	0-0	
21 Mar	(h)	Roma	1-0	*Graziani*
28 Mar	(a)	Juventus	2-0	*og 2*
4 Apr	(h)	Milan	2-1	*Graziani, Garritano*
11 Apr	(a)	Como	1-0	*Graziani*
18 Apr	(h)	Fiorentina	4-3	*Pulici 3, Zaccarelli*
25 Apr	(a)	Lazio	1-1	*C. Sala*
2 May	(h)	Cagliari	5-1	*Pecci, Graziani, Zaccarelli, Pulici 2*
9 May	(a)	Verona	0-0	
16 May	(h)	Cesena	1-1	*Pulici*

	Apps	*Goals*
Bacchin	1	
Caporale	28	
Castellini	29	
Cazzaniga R.	3	
Garritano	5	1
Gorin II	12	1
Graziani	29	15
Lombardo	3	
Mozzini	29	
Pallavicini	4	
Pecci	29	2
Pulici	30	21
Sala C.	29	1
Sala P.	30	
Salvadori	30	
Santin	25	
Zaccarelli	28	4
Own-goals		4

La Classifica

			Home			Away			Total					
		P	W	D	L	W	D	L	W	D	L	F	A	Pts
1.	Torino	30	14	1	0	4	8	3	18	9	3	49	22	45
2.	Juventus	30	10	4	1	8	3	4	18	7	5	46	26	43
3.	Milan	30	9	3	3	6	5	4	15	8	7	42	28	38
4.	Inter	30	11	3	1	3	6	6	14	9	7	36	28	37
5.	Napoli	30	8	5	2	5	5	5	13	10	7	40	27	36
6.	Cesena	30	7	6	2	2	8	5	9	14	7	39	35	32
7.	Bologna	30	6	7	2	3	7	5	9	14	7	32	32	32
8.	Perugia	30	8	6	1	2	5	8	10	11	9	31	34	31
9.	Fiorentina	30	5	5	5	4	4	7	9	9	12	39	39	27
10.	Roma	30	3	9	3	3	4	8	6	13	11	25	31	25
11.	Verona	30	6	5	4	2	3	10	8	8	14	35	46	24
12.	Sampdoria	30	7	2	6	1	6	8	8	8	14	21	32	24
13.	Lazio	30	5	7	3	1	4	10	6	11	13	35	40	23
14.	Ascoli	30	4	8	3	0	7	8	4	15	11	19	34	23
15.	Como	30	4	7	4	1	4	10	5	11	14	28	36	21
16.	Cagliari	30	4	5	6	1	4	10	5	9	16	25	52	19

The Scudetto Line-ups

1927-28
Bosia, Martin III (Vicenzi), Martin II, Martin I, Colombari, Sperone, Vezzani, Baloncieri, Libonatti, Rossetti, Franzoni.
Coach: Schoffer.

1942-43
Bodoira, Piacentini, Ferrini, Baldi, Ellena, Grezar, Menti, Loik, Gabetto, Mazzola, Ferraris II.
Coach: Kutik (later Janni).

1945-46
Bacigalupo, Ballarin, Maroso, Grezar, Rigamonti, Castigliano, Ossola, Loik,Gabetto, Mazzola, Ferraris II.
Coach: Ferrero.

1946-47, champions of Italy. From left to right (standing): Castigliano, Maroso, Rigamonti, Grezar, Bacigalupo, Ballarin, Ferraris. Sitting: Mazzola, Ossola, Loik, Gabetto.

1946-47
Bacigalupo, Ballarin, Maroso, Grezar, Rigamonti, Castigliano, Ossola, Loik, Gabetto, Mazzola, Ferraris II.
Coaches: Cargnelli and Ferrero.

1947-48

Bacigalupo, Ballarin, Toma (Maroso), Grezar, Rigamonti, Castigliano (Martelli), Menti, Loik, Gabetto, Mazzola, Ossola.

Coach: Sperone.

1948-49, champions of Italy. From left to right (standing): Castigliano, Ballarin, Rigamonti, Loik, Maroso, Mazzola. Sitting: Bacigalupo, Menti, Ossola, Martelli, Gabetto.

1948-49

Bacigalupo, Ballarin, Maroso, Grezar (Martelli), Rigamonti, Castigliano, Menti, Loik, Gabetto, Mazzola, Ossola.
Coach: Lievesley.

1975-76

Castellini, Santin, Salvadori, P. Sala, Mozzini, Caporale, C. Sala, Pecci, Graziani, Zaccarelli, Pulici.
Coach: Radice.

The Coppa Italia Line-ups

1935-36

Maina, Brunella, Ferrini, Gallea, Janni, Prato, Bo, Baldi III, Galli II, Buscaglia, Silano.
Coach: Cargnelli.

1942-43

Bodoira, Piacentini, Ferrini, Gallea, Ellena, Grezar, Ossola, Loik, Gabetto, Mazzola, Ferraris II.
Coach: Janni

The Grande Torino, 1942-43, from left: Mazzola, Ellena, Ossola, Baldi, Gabetto, Gallea, Menti, Ferrini, Loik, Piacentini, Ferraris, Cavalli, Grezar, Bodoira and Janni (coach).

1967-68
Vieri, Fossati, Trebbi, Puia, Cereser, Agroppi, Carelli (Corni), Ferrini, Combin, Moschino, Facchin. Coach: Fabbri.

1970-71
Castellini, Poletti, Fossati, Puia, Cereser, Agroppi, Rampanti, Ferrini, Petrini (Madde), Sala, Luppi. Coach: Cade.

1992-93
Marchegiani, Bruno, Mussi, Fortunato, Cois, Fusi, Sordo (Falcone), Venturin, Aguilera (Casagrande), Scifo, Silenzi. Coach: Mondonico.

Il Grande Torino Five-year Scudetto Record

	P	W	D	L	F	A	
1942-43	30	20	4	6	68	31	
1945-46	26	19	4	3	65	18	(Alta Italia)
1945-46	14	11	0	3	43	14	(Final Stage)
1946-47	38	28	7	3	104	35	
1947-48	40	29	7	4	125	33	
1948-49	38	25	10	3	78	34	
Total	186	132	32	22	483	165	

Career Profiles of Il Grande Torino

(players who died at Superga)

Valerio Bacigalupo

Birthplace: Vado Ligure (SV) 12 March 1924
Position: Goalkeeper

Previous clubs: Cairese, Savona, Genoa

Debut in Serie A for Grande Torino: 14 October 1945: Juventus-Torino 2-1
Appearances and goals for Grande Torino: 137-115
Debut in national team: 14 December 1947: Italy-Czechoslovakia 3-1
Appearance and goals for national team: 5-8

Season	Team	Serie	Apps	Gls
1941-42	Cairese	1	Div	
1942-43	Savona	B	20	-
1944	Genoa		(1)	
1945-46	Torino	A	40	-
1946-47	Torino	A	25	-
1947-48	Torino	A	40	-
1948-49	Torino	A	32	-

Aldo Ballarin

Birthplace: Chioggia (VE), 10 January 1922
Position: Full-back
Previous clubs: Rovigo, Triestina, Venezia
Debut in Serie A: 26 October 1941: Triestina-Lazio 0-0
Debut in Serie A for Grande Torino: 14 October 1945: Juventus-Torino 2-1
Appearances and goals for Grande Torino: 148-4
Debut in national team: 11 November 1945: Switzerland-Italy 4-4
Appearances and goals for national team: 9-0

Season	Team	Serie	Apps	Gls
1940-41	Rovigo	C	-	-
1941-42	Triestina	A	-	
1942-43	Triestina	A		

1944	Venezia		(3)	
1945-46	Torino	A	39	2
1946-47	Torino	A	38	-
1947-48	Torino	A	39	1
1948-49	Torino	A	32	1

The Grande Torino 1948-49. Back row, left to right: Castigliano, Ballarin, Rigamonti, Loik, Maroso, Mazzola. Front row: Bacigalupo, Menti, Ossola, Martelli, Gabetto.

Dino Ballarin

Birthplace: Chioggia (VE), 11 December 1925
Position: Goalkeeper
Previous clubs: Chioggia

Season	Team	Serie	Apps	Gls
1947-48	Chioggia	Dil	-	-
1948-49	Torino	A	-	-

Emile Bongiorni

Birthplace: Boulogne-Billancourt (France), 19 March 1921
Position: Centre-forward-Wing back
Previous clubs: CAP Paris, Racing Club de Paris
Debut in Serie A for Grande Torino: 19 December 1948: Fiorentina-Torino 0-0
Appearances and goals for Grande Torino: 8-2

Season	Team	Serie	Apps	Gls
1948-49	Torino	A	8	2

Eusebio Castigliano

Birthplace: Vercelli, 9 February 1921
Position: Midfield
Previous clubs: Pro Vercelli, Biellese, Lecco, Spezia
Debut in Serie A for Grande Torino: 14 October 1945: Juventus-Torino 2-1
Appearances and goals for Grande Torino: 116-35
Debut in national team: 11 November 1945: Switzerland-Italy 4-4
Appearances and goals for national team: 7-1

Season	Team	Serie	Apps	Gls
1939-40	Pro Vercelli	B	9	6
1940-41	Pro Vercelli	B		
1941-42	Spezia	B	33	17
1942-43	Spezia	B	29	8
1944	Biellese	1		
1945	Lecco	5		
1945-46	Torino	A	39	19
1946-47	Torino	A	27	8
1947-48	Torino	A	29	7
1948-49	Torino	A	21	1

Rubens Fadini

Birthplace: Jolanda di Savoia (FE), 1 June 1927
Position: Midfield-Wing back
Previous clubs: Ceretti, Tanfani, Gallaratese
Debut in Serie A for Grande Torino: 7 November 1948: Torino-Lazio 1-0
Appearances and goals for Grande Torino: 10-1

Season	Team	Serie	Apps	Gls
1945-46	Gallaratese	B		
1946-47	Gallaratese	B	15	-
1947-48	Gallaratese	B	30	-
1948-49	Torino	A	10	1

Guglielmo Gabetto

Birthplace: Turin, 24 February 1916
Position: Centre-forward
Previous club: Juventus
Debut in Serie A: 27 January 1935: Pro Vercelli-Juventus 0-1
Debut in Serie A for Torino: 2 November 1941: Lazio-Torino 4-1
First appearance for Grande Torino: 4 October 1942: Ambrosiana-Torino 1-0
Appearances and goals for Torino: 225-125
Debut in national team: 5 April 1942: Italy-Croatia 4-0
Appearances and goals for national team: 6-5

Season	Team	Serie	Apps	Gls
1934-35	Juventus	A	6	-
1935-36	Juventus	A	22	20
1936-37	Juventus	A	30	17
1937-38	Juventus	A	22	9
1938-39	Juventus	A	27	10
1939-40	Juventus	A	29	12

1944, The Torino-Fiat. From left to right (standing): Janni (coach), Cadario, Piacentini, Griffanti, Mazzola, Ferraris, Gallea. Sitting: Cassano, Ossola, Ellena, Piola, Gabetto.

1940-41	Juventus	A	28	16
1941-42	Torino	A	27	16
1942-43	Torino	A	26	14
1944	Torino	1	26	18
1945-46	Torino	A	35	22
1946-47	Torino	A	35	19
1947-48	Torino	A	36	23
1948-49	Torino	A	34	8

The Grande Torino, 1946-47.

Ruggero Grava

Birthplace: Claut (UD), 26 April 1922
Position: Centre- forward
Previous club: Roubaix
Debut in Serie for Grande Torino: 26 December 1948: Genoa-Torino 3-0
Appearances and goals for Grande Torino: 1-0

Season	Team	Serie	Apps	Gls
1948-49	Torino	A	1	-

Giuseppe Grezar

Birthplace: Trieste, 25 November 1918
Position: Midfield
Previous clubs: Ampelea, Triestina
Debut in Serie A: 17 September 1939; Triestina-Novara 2-0
Debut in Serie A for Grande Torino: 4 October 1942: Ambrosiana-Torino 1-0
Appearances and goals for Grande Torino: 159-19
Debut in national team: 5 April 1942: Italy-Czechoslovakia 4-0
Appearances and goals for national team: 8-1 (Triestina 1-1, Torino 7-0)

Season	Team	Serie	Apps	Gls
1938-39	Triestina	A	-	-
1939-40	Triestina	A	27	6
1940-41	Triestina	A	28	6
1941-42	Triestina	A	28	3
1942-43	Torino	A	30	3
1944	Ampelea		(4)	
1945-46	Torino	A	35	4
1946-47	Torino	A	35	4
1947-48	Torino	A	33	5
1948-49	Torino	A	21	3

1945-46, champions of Italy. From left to right (standing): Castigliano, Maroso, Grezar, Ballarin, Mazzola, Ferraris. Sitting: Loik, Bacigalupo, Rigamonti, Gabetto, Ossola.

Ezio Loik

Birthplace: Fiume, 26 September 1919
Position: Wing back
Previous clubs: Fiumana, Milan, Venezia
Debut in Serie A: 16 January 1938: Liguria-Milan 1-1
Debut in Serie A for Grande Torino: 4 October 1942: Ambrosiana-Torino 1-0
Appearances and goals for Grande Torino: 181-72
Debut in national team: 5 April 1942: Italy-Croatia 4-0
Appearances and goals in national team: 9-4 (Venezia 2-1, Torino 7-3)

Season	Team	Serie	Apps	Gls
1936-37	Fiumana	(C)		
1937-38	Milan	A	2	1
1938-39	Milan	A	21	4
1939-40	Milan	A	30	5
1940-41	Venezia	A	30	7
1941-42	Venezia	A	30	6
1942-43	Torino	A	30	9
1944	Torino	1	16	8
1945-46	Torino	A	39	16
1946-47	Torino	A	30	12
1947-48	Torino	A	33	16
1948-49	Torino	A	28	9

Virgilio Maroso

Birthplace: Crosara di Marostica (VI), 26 June 1925
Position: Full-back
Previous club: Alessandria
Debut in Serie A for Grande Torino: 14 October 1945: Juventus-Torino 2-1
Appearances and goals for Grande Torino: 103-1
Debut in national team: 11 November 1945: Switzerland-Italy 4-4
Appearances and goals for national team: 7-1

Season	Team	Serie	Apps	Gls
1942-43	Torino	A		
1944	Alessandria		(1)	
1945-46	Torino	A	35	
1946-47	Torino	A	33	
1947-48	Torino	A	17	1
1948-49	Torino	A	18	

Danilo Martelli

Birthplace: Castellucchio (MN), 27 May 1923
Position: Midfield-Wing back
Previous clubs: Marzotto, Brescia
Debut in Serie A: 14 October 1945: Atalanta-Brescia 0-0
Debut in Serie A for Grande Torino: 20 October 1946: Torino-Juventus 0-0
Appearances and goals for Grande Torino: 72-10

Season	Team	Serie	Apps	Gls
1940-41	Marzotto	C		
1941-42	Brescia	B	33	13
1942-43	Brescia	B	31	8

1945-46	Brescia	A	25	-
1946-47	Torino	A	17	1
1947-48	Torino	A	27	9
1948-49	Torino	A	28	

Valentino Mazzola

Birthplace: Cassano d'Adda (MI), 26 January 1919
Position: Wing back
Previous clubs: Tresoldi, Alfa Romeo, Venezia
Debut in Serie A: 31 March 1940: Lazio-Venezia 1-0
Debut in Serie A for Grande Torino: 4 October 1942; Ambrosiana-Torino 1-0
Appearances and goals for Grande Torino: 200-123
Debut in national team: 5 April 1942: Italy-Croatia 4-0
Appearances and goals in national team: 12-4 (Venezia 2-1, Torino 10-3)

Season	Team	Serie	Apps	Gls
1938-39	Alfa Romeo	C		
1939-40	Venezia	A	6	1
1940-41	Venezia	A	27	6
1941-42	Venezia	A	28	5
1942-43	Torino	A	30	11
1944	Torino	1	25	21
1945-46	Torino	A	35	16
1946-47	Torino	A	38	29
1947-48	Torino	A	37	25
1948-49	Torino	A	30	16

Romeo Menti

Birthplace: Vicenza, 5 September 1919
Position: Winger
Previous clubs: Vicenza, Milan, Fiorentina
Debut in Serie A: 17 September 1939: Fiorentina-Genoa 1-1
Debut for Torino: 26 October 1941: Torino-Liguria 3-2
First match for Grande Torino: 4 October 1942: Ambrosiana-Torino 1-0
Appearances and goals for Torino: 133-53
Debut in national team: 27 April 1947: Italy-Switzerland 5-2
Appearances and goals for national team: 7-5

Season	Team	Serie	Apps	Gls
1934-35	Vicenza	B	3	
1935-36	Vicenza	C		
1936-37	Vicenza	C		
1937-38	Vicenza	C		
1938-39	Fiorentina	B	29	17
1939-40	Fiorentina	A	17	9
1940-41	Fiorentina	A	29	18
1941-42	Torino	A	28	14
1942-43	Torino	A	22	8
1944	Milan		(2)	
1945-46	Fiorentina	A	18	7
1946-47	Torino	A	14	6
1947-48	Torino	A	38	16
1948-49	Torino	A	29	9

Pierino Operto

Birthplace: Turin, 20 December 1926
Position: Full-back
Previous clubs: Piedmont, Casale
Debut in Serie A for Grande Torino: 30 October 1948: Torino-Roma 4-0
Appearances and goals for Grande Torino: 11-0

Season	Team	Serie	Apps	Gls
1946-47	Casale	B	41	-
1947-48	Casale	C		
1948-49	Torino	A	11	-

Franco Ossola

Birthplace: Varese, 23 August 1921
Position: Winger
Previous clubs: Varese
Debut in Serie A for Torino: 4 February 1940: Novara-Torino 0-1
First appearance for Grande Torino: 11 October 1942: Torino-Livorno 1-2
Appearances and goals for Torino: 182-91

Season	Team	Serie	Apps	Gls
1938-39	Varese	C	9	3
1939-40	Torino	A	4	-
1940-41	Torino	A	22	15
1941-42	Torino	A	13	7
1942-43	Torino	A	12	6
1944	Torino	1	24	14
1945-46	Torino	A	30	11
1946-47	Torino	A	29	13
1947-48	Torino	A	17	9
1948-49	Torino	A	25	11

Mario Rigamonti

Birthplace: Brescia, 17 December 1922
Position: Stopper
Previous clubs: Lecco, Brescia
Debut in Serie A for Grande Torino: 14 October 1945: Juventus-Torino 2-1
Appearances and goals for Grande Torino: 140-1
Debut in national team: 11 May 1947: Italy-Hungary 3-2
Appearances and goals for national team: 3-0

Season	Team	Serie	Apps	Gls
1940-41	Brescia	B	-	-
1941-42	Torino	A	-	-
1942-43	Torino	A	-	-
1944	Brescia		(2)	
1945	Lecco		(5)	
1945-46	Torino	A	36	-
1946-47	Torino	A	34	-
1947-48	Torino	A	39	-
1948-49	Torino	A	31	1

Julius Schubert

Birthplace: Budapest (Hungary), 12 December 1922
Position: wing-half
Previous club: AK Bratislava
Debut in Serie A for Grande Torino: 6 January 1949: Palermo-Torino 2-2
Appearances and goals for Grande Torino: 5-1

Note. The 1944 Alta Italia war championship was not officially recognised by the Football Federation and various tournaments were played.
(1) Championship Liguria-Piedmont
(2) Championship Lombardo
(3) Championship Veneto
(4) Championship Giuliano
(5) Tournament of Benefico Lombardo

In some instances of the career profiles, records of appearances and goals are not available, particularly relating to the War Championship. The above figures have therefore been compiled as comprehensively as possible.

Il Grande Torino in the Italian National Team

Genoa, 5 Apr 1942, Italy v Croatia 4-0
2 players: Ferraris (1), Gabetto (1)

Milan 19 Apr 1942, Italy v Spain 4-0
1 player: Ferraris (1)

Zurich 11 Nov 1945, Switzerland v Italy 4-4
7 players: Ballarin, Maroso, Mazzola, Grezar, Castigliano, Ferraris, Loik

Milan 1 Dec 1946, Italy v Austria 3-2
5 players: Maroso, Grezar, Ferraris, Mazzola (1), Castigliano (1)

Florence, 27 Apr 1947, Italy v Switzerland 5-2
9 players: Castigliano, Ballarin, Gabetto, Maroso, Grezar, Loik (1), Menti (3), Mazzola (1), Ferraris

Turin, 11 May 1947, Italy v Hungary 3-2
10 players: Ballarin, Maroso, Rigamonti, Grezar, Castigliano, Menti, Mazzola, Ferraris, Gabetto (2), Loik (1)

Vienna, 9 Nov 1947, Austria v Italy 5-1
4 players: Ballarin, Maroso, Mazzola, Castigliano

Bari, 14 Dec 1947, Italy v Czechoslovakia 3-1
8 players: Bacigalupo, Ballarin, Grezar, Maroso, Loik, Mazzola, Menti (1), Gabetto (1)

Paris, 4 Apr 1948, France v Italy 1-3
8 players: Bacigalupo, Ballarin, Loik, Grezar, Rigamonti, Menti, Mazzola, Gabetto (1)

Turin, 16 May 1948, Italy v England 0-4
7 players: Bacigalupo, Ballarin, Grezar, Menti, Loik, Gabetto, Mazzola

Genoa, 27 Feb 1949, Italy v Portugal 4-1
7 players: Bacigalupo, Ballarin, Loik, Maroso (1), Castigliano, Menti (1), Mazzola (1)

Madrid, 27 Mar 1949, Spain v Italy 1-3
6 players: Bacigalupo, Ballarin, Rigamonti, Castigliano, Menti, Mazzola

Appearances (Goals)
Mazzola 10 (3), Ballarin 9, Grezar 7, Maroso 7 (1), Menti 7 (5), Loik 7 (3), Castigliano 7 (1), Gabetto 6 (5), Ferraris II 6 (2), Bacigalupo 5 (-8), Rigamonti 3.

Winners of the Italian Championship

1898	Genoa		1949-50	Juventus
1899	Genoa		1950-51	Milan
1900	Genoa		1951-52	Juventus
1901	Milan		1952-53	Inter
1902	Genoa		1953-54	Inter
1903	Genoa		1954-55	Milan
1904	Genoa		1955-56	Fiorentina
1905	Juventus		1956-57	Milan
1906	Milan		1957-58	Juventus
1907	Milan		1958-59	Milan
1908	Pro Vercelli		1959-60	Juventus
1909	Pro Vercelli		1960-61	Juventus
1909-10	Inter		1961-62	Milan
1910-11	Pro Vercelli		1962-63	Inter
1911-12	Pro Vercelli		1963-64	Bologna
1912-13	Pro Vercelli		1964-65	Inter
1913-14	Casale		1965-66	Inter
1914-15	Genoa		1966-67	Juventus
1916-19	Suspended due to World War One		1967-68	Milan
	Replaced in 1915-16 by the Coppa		1968-69	Fiorentina
	Federale won by Milan		1969-70	Cagliari
1919-20	Inter		1970-71	Inter
1920-21	Pro Vercelli		1971-72	Juventus
1921-22	Pro Vercelli (Champions CCI)		1972-73	Juventus
	Novese (Champions FIGC)		1973-74	Lazio
1922-23	Genoa		1974-75	Juventus
1923-24	Genoa		1975-76	Torino
1924-25	Bologna		1976-77	Juventus
1925-26	Juventus		1977-78	Juventus
1926-27	Torino (revoked)		1978-79	Milan
1927-28	Torino		1979-80	Inter
1928-29	Bologna		1980-81	Juventus
1929-30	Ambrosiana-Inter		1981-82	Juventus
1930-31	Juventus		1982-83	Roma
1931-32	Juventus		1983-84	Juventus
1932-33	Juventus		1984-85	Verona
1933-34	Juventus		1985-86	Juventus
1934-35	Juventus		1986-87	Napoli
1935-36	Bologna		1987-88	Milan
1936-37	Bologna		1988-89	Inter
1937-38	Ambrosiana-Inter		1989-90	Napoli
1938-39	Bologna		1990-91	Sampdoria
1939-40	Ambrosiana-Inter		1991-92	Milan
1940-41	Bologna		1992-93	Milan
1941-42	Roma		1993-94	Milan
1942-43	Torino		1994-95	Juventus
1944	War Championship.		1995-96	Milan
	Winners La Spezia were not		1996-97	Juventus
	officialy recognised by the		1997-98	Juventus
	Football Federation.		1998-99	Milan
1945-46	Torino		1999-2000	Lazio
1946-47	Torino			
1947-48	Torino			
1948-49	Torino			

Index

Index

ND - #0283 - 270225 - C0 - 234/156/13 - PB - 9781780914800 - Gloss Lamination